The Beatification of Area Boy
A Lagosian Kaleidoscope

An opulent shopping plaza and a street lined with makeshift stalls. Lagos. Amid the scenes of everyday racketeering, general hubbub and disquiet, the police try to clear the area of undesirables. A traditional wedding between two illustrious and ambitious families is about to take place at the plaza . . .

Wole Soyinka was born in Nigeria in 1934. Educated there and at Leeds University, he worked in British theatre before returning to Nigeria in 1960. In 1986, he became the first African writer to win the Nobel Price for Literature. His plays include *The Jero Plays* (1960, 1966), *The Road* (1965), *The Lion and the Jewel* (1966), *Madmen and Specialists* (1971), *Death and the King's Horseman* (1975), *A Play with Giants* (1984), *A Scourge of Hyacinths* (1991) and *From Zia, With Love* (1992). His novels include *The Interpreters* (1973) and *Season of Anomy* (1980) and his collections of poetry include *Idanre* (1967), *A Shuttle in the Crypt* (1972), composed during a period of over two years in prison without trial, most of it in solitary confinement; and *Mandela's Earth* (1990). In 1988, his collection of essays on literature and culture, *Art, Dialogue and Outrage*, was published. He has also written three autobiographical volumes *Aké: The Years of Childhood* (1981), *Ìsarà: A Voyage Around Essay* (1989) and *Ibadan* (1994).

Wole Soyinka

THE BEATIFICATION OF AREA BOY
A Lagosian Kaleidoscope

METHUEN DRAMA

Methuen Drama **Modern Plays**

First published in Great Britain 1995
by Methuen Drama

ISBN 0–413–68680–9

A CIP catalogue record for this book
is available from the British Library

Typeset by Wilmaset Ltd, Birkenhead, Wirral

THE BEATIFICATION OF AREA BOY

A Lagosian Kaleidoscope

CHARACTERS

JUDGE
TRADER (AREA TWO-ONE)
BARBER
SHOP WORKER
SANDA (OGA SECURITY)
MAMA PUT
BOYKO
MINSTREL
GIRL, *Mama Put's daughter*
CYCLIST
BIG MAN SHOPPER
FOREIGNER
PARKING ATTENDANT
AREA TWO-FOUR
NEWSVENDOR
MISEYI (BRIDE)
MAID
POLICE
ACCUSED
VICTIM
WITNESS
ANOTHER WITNESS
WOMAN
CONDUCTOR (*voice only*)
PASSENGER
WARDER
PRISONER 1
PRISONER 2
MILITARY OFFICER
ADC
SOLDIER
MILITARY GOVERNOR
BAND LEADER

ADC *to Military Governor*
BRIDEGROOM
CHIEF KINGBOLI, *Bridegroom's father*
MASTER OF CEREMONIES
MOTHER OF THE DAY

Guests, Musicians, Major-Domo, Caterers, Soldiers etc.

ACKNOWLEDGEMENTS . . .

. . . to participants in the 'ITI/Sisi Clara' Master Workshop of 1992 where parts of some scenes of *The Beatification of Area Boy* were developed, especially to the old hands from Orisun Theatre – Tunji Oyelana, Yewande Johnson (née Akinbo), Yomi Obileye, Wale Ogunyemi – plus Charles Mike from the Artistes' Collective, Lagos.

NOTE

Certain Yoruba words which appear in italics in the text are explained in a glossary at the back of the book together with a translation of the song on pages 65–67.

The broad frontage of an opulent shopping plaza. Early daybreak. As the day becomes brighter, the broad sliding doors of tinted glass will reflect (and distort) traffic scenes from the main street which would seem to run through the rear of the auditorium. This is realised by projections, using the sliding doors as uneven screens. When the doors slide open, the well-stocked interior of consumer items – a three-dimensional projection or photo blow-up will suffice – contrast vividly with the slummy exterior.

Frontstage consists of a broad pavement, with three or four broad steps leading up to it. An alleyway along the right side of the shopping block vanishes into the rear, and is lined by the usual makeshift stalls, vending their assortment of snacks, cigarettes, soft drinks, household goods, wearing apparel, cheap jewellery etc. The closest stall to the street, downstage right corner of the block, belongs to TRADER, *also addressed as* AREA TWO-ONE. *He is busy arranging his stall which soon displays a wide assortment of cheap consumer goods. The barber-stall will be to the left, next to* MAMA PUT's *food corner.*

A partially covered drainage runs in front of the shopping block. Street-level planks laid across the gutter provide a crossing into the alleyway.

A vagrant, called JUDGE, *is perched on a step near the top. His posture suggests some kind of yoga-type body exercise.*

JUDGE. I breathed into the sky before I slept, and – just look at the result.

TRADER. Enh? Oh, good morning, your lordship.

JUDGE. It's a good display, not so? And to think all I did was breathe against the horizon. It was the last exhalation before I lay down – emptying all the secret spaces of my body – (*Gently presses his fingertips against chest, stomach and sides.*) – I had completed my nightly exercises – yoga – do you practise yoga at all?

TRADER. Yo – ga?

JUDGE. I knew it was a good exhalation, deep and purifying. All the day's anxieties and violence – mostly other people's – gathered into one breath. (*Pressing his belly upwards to his chest.*) This is where it gets transformed, and there it all is, spread across the sky. To look at it, you'd never guess what went through my alimentary canal, into the arteries and lungs. But I'm used to it. Even if I sometimes feel like the city's sewage system . . . or its kidneys – most of the purification is done in the kidneys you know . . . the city is all the better for it. Nothing like starting a new day on a clean slate.

TRADER. Oh, that na good idea. That must to feel very good for you, Judge. Na only kind man like you go think of others before you go sleep.

JUDGE. If we don't remit sentences from time to time, the gaols will be full. The entire city, the nation itself, will become one huge prison camp. That is why we have a council for the prerogative of mercy. I have not formally enrolled but . . . (*Points at the sky.*) Isn't it amazing what an individual can do on his own? Have you applied? Of course you'll be on the receiving end.

TRADER (*slight impatience, under his breath*). Other people, when they wake up for morning time just dey pray. Simple prayer, 'e do them. Dis one . . . I done tire!

JUDGE. You musn't tire. Never give up. You apply the first time, they turn you down, you try and try again. I was rejected six times you know. When I was like you, on the receiving end.

TRADER. Na so?

JUDGE. Finally, I wore them down with my petitions. Last night, it was finally granted.

TRADER. Congratulations, your lordship. Congratulations.

JUDGE. I signed the letter myself, for the avoidance of doubt. I know the format. Afterwards you wonder, why hadn't I thought of it all these years? Those who decide Yes or No, they are mere mortals, aren't they? And mostly on an inferior plane of awareness, I have written many petitions in my time for clients, and I know the standard responses. One for rejection, the other approval. This time, mine was . . .

TRADER. Approved.

JUDGE. Oh. How did you know?

TRADER. Na you tell me yourself, now now.

JUDGE (*suspicious*). Did you see the letter?

TRADER. Even if to say I did, I fit read. Look, na early morning. I dey prepare for my customers and I wan' think small. We currency done fall again, petrol dey scarcity, which mean to say, transport fare done double. As for foodstuff and other commodity, even gari wey be poor man diet . . . (*Stops as he observes* JUDGE *looking at him with total mystification.*) I just dey explain why I need small time to put new price for all dese goods. (JUDGE *looks even more bewildered.*) Look, no to this time you begin walka for your circuit . . . er . . . circuit court or wetin you dey call am?

JUDGE. The courts will not sit today, so I am master of my time.

TRADER (*groans*). You mean na here you go siddon all day?

JUDGE. No. Today I start on a different journey. I begin the long journey to the kingdom of lost souls. I shall relieve them of their torment.

TRADER (*looks him up and down*). You go need a pair of shoes then.

JUDGE. What?

TRADER. A strong pair of shoes. It sound like long journey. You no fit afford the bus fare.

JUDGE (*at his most supercilious*). I do not recall addressing you. I am not aware that the accused was given leave to address the court.

TRADER. Aha! I done catch you. You no fit start dat one with me today. Who you dey talk to all this time then? Na only two of us dey here.

JUDGE. You see? You should always rely on your counsel. You think you see only two of us but in fact, there are three. Or four. Strictly I should say three but I am giving you the benefit of the doubt. In any case, I was actually addressing my soul, not yours, or you. Ha-ha, any good counsel would have saved you from that trap.

TRADER. Addressing which kin' soul? You no fit use telephone either. And as I see am, the way I bin know you all these years, na long distance call if you want talk to your soul. Expensive.

JUDGE. That's the way it must appear to the soulless.

TRADER. Or inside dustbin. The way you search every morning inside dustbin and refuse dump . . .

JUDGE. For evidence, fool, for vital clues. If the police don't do their work, then the court must search out the truth wherever it may be hidden. I am not one of your sedentary ministers of truth, friend. I did not opt for the circuit courts for nothing, declining even secondment to the Supreme Court. But it's all there in my curriculum vitae – if you care to read it. Or had the ability to read.

TRADER. Thank you. I no fit read, but I sabbe the world pass you. Even Mama Put's small pickin talk sense pass you – make you go preach to am.

> JUDGE *rises, stretches himself, then lowers his body and does one or two contortions. Stops. His gaze becomes riveted on the sky.*

JUDGE. It is the kind of day when unbelievers are shamed and the faithful exalted. Look at that horizon – there, where the sun is just rising. Have you ever seen a dawn the likes of that? (*Grandly.*) Do you see how it's opening up the rest of the sky? My work. Pity I slept late, so I could not usher it in with the secret mantras. Still, asleep or awake, that dawn is my handiwork.

TRADER (*straining to see*). Dawn? Which kin' dawn? I only see the sun wey begin expose all those dirty roofs for Isale-eko. Na so e dey do am every morning. Wetin get special about his one? And wetin concern you sun for sun and sky? The *wahala* wey you get for this earth no do you?

JUDGE. I am a specialist of sunrise. I have seen more dawns from every vantage point, more dawns than you can count white hairs on my head. I have a proprietary feeling towards dawns you see, not that you can understand but, I have a right to claim that they belong to me. Once, I could only predict what kind of sunrise it would be, yes, I could tell that even before going to sleep. Then I began to pray for the kind of dawn into which I wanted to wake. In detail, you know. Colours. Moods. Shapes. Shades of stillness or motion. It was something to look forward to.

TRADER. It mus' to help take your mind off those mosquitoes. Or rough weather. Person wey go sleep on empty stomach must take sometin' fill in mind. Otherwise, how 'e go fit sleep?

JUDGE. Oh Trader, Trader. Because you see a lifeless form here or in a dark alleyway with ravenous rats for companion, yes, and on the beach sometimes, or in the back of a derelict lorry, a form that wears my face, do you really think my soul will be found within that form?

TRADER. Excuse me o. No vex with me. I think say na you I come dey meet here every morning when I come prepare for the day's business.

JUDGE. You'll never know what it is to wake into day on the rooftops – yes, those rooftops you call dirty – to wake up on the skyline face to face with every day a different face of itself, just as your mind had painted it before you fell asleep. If you prayed hard enough. When I still prayed – and that was a while ago. Because – it's all a matter of self-development, training you know – I began to dispense with prayers. I took charge. I began to make dawns to order.

TRADER. Yeah? You find plenty customer?

JUDGE (*pitying look*). Of course. I forget, you have the mind of a petty commercial.

TRADER. It feeds me you know, it feeds me. I'm not complaining.

JUDGE. How can you complain when you know no better. Nor aspire to something better. (*Looks up sharply in the direction of the sunrise.*) You have wasted enough of my time . . .

TRADER. I have what?!

JUDGE. Wasted too much of my time. By now I should have been foraging in the disposal sector of that new nightclub – yes, The New Lagoon. No matter, when I encounter you again in the morning, you will find I have gone professional.

TRADER. Professional? Doing what?

JUDGE. Doing what I have finally accepted I was meant for. My head is clear on that score. As clear as that sky you see blossoming before my presence . . . yes, my journey to the kingdom of souls begins today. People say the nation has lost its soul but that is nonsense. It's all a matter of finding out where it's hidden. (*Stops, reflects.*) Unless it never had any? Is that possible? No! I have hesitated too long. The route is clearly along the prerogative of mercy. Once I thought it lay along the trail of the majesty of the law but – well, one had to begin somewhere. We grow, we develop . . . (*Goes off, mumbling.*)

TRADER (*shakes his head, sadly*). I go miss am. The day they take am commot here and lock him up, I go miss am too much.

BARBER (*entering*). Who will you miss?

TRADER. Oh. Good morning. You no pass each other?

BARBER. Oh, it's that one. Is he relocating?

TRADER. Who sabbe for am? Today na business of dawn and sunrise. And he say he wan' go professional.

BARBER (*looks up*). Ah, you must admit it's a spectacular one. I noticed it myself as soon as I opened my window.

TRADER. Oh, you too.

BARBER. Me too?

TRADER. All I sabbe na say the morning begin show the pothole and garbage before in normal time. Before before, I no dey see them on my way here. Today 'e get bright so early, I tink say na different street I take reach here.

BARBER. It's still a colourful sky to wake up to. And you can hardly blame it for the refuse dumps, can you? If the town council won't clear them, what can even God do about it?

He sets about preparing his barber-stall. Rolls the plastic cover from the swivel chair. Ties on an off-white apron. Spreads a white cloth over a half-drum on which he then arranges his combs, clippers, scissors, hair lotions etc.

A SHOP WORKER *in the plaza arrives, bids good morning to the two, then looks around, puzzled.*

SHOP WORKER. No one arrive yet? Have you seen Security?

BARBER (*exchanges puzzled looks with* TRADER). But you are early. None of your people ever gets here until at least thirty minutes after I've set up for business. Only Trader gets here before me.

TRADER. You no dey use alarm clock?

SHOP WORKER. Me? I no get watch self.

TRADER. How you dey get to work then? You no dey come late?

SHOP WORKER. Never. As soon as I open my eyes and look outside, I can tell the time.

BARBER (*to* TRADER). You see. Didn't I tell you? That sunrise must have fooled her. I bet it fooled half of Lagos.

TRADER. Abi you wan buy alarm clock? For next time. Make you open the day's palm for me and I go give you good discount.

SHOP WORKER. I beg, leave me. Look how I bin run come work instead of chopping my breakfast jejely. I tink say I done late so much, dem go sack me.

Sits down on pavement in annoyance.

Enter MAMA PUT, *preceded by* BOYKO *carrying all her cooking utensils etc. He assists in setting up her corner. The cooking fires are lit, bowls and plates stacked. He goes off with a pail and returns later with it filled with water. General preparation for business.* BOYKO *alternates between helping her and* TRADER, *practising on a small flute when he is unoccupied with either.* SANDA *corrects his false notes in an indulgent manner.*

TRADER. You late small today, Mama Put.

MAMA PUT. I no feel well at all. But for say I no wan' disappoint my customers, I no for commot house at all.

BARBER. Wes matter?

MAMA PUT. I no know. No to say my body no feel well, na the day inself no look well. I commot for house and I nearly go back and stay inside house. I no like the face of today, dat na God's truth. Make you just look that sky. E dey like animal wey just chop in victim, with blood dripping from in wide open mouth.

TRADER. A be you dream bad dream again last night?

MAMA PUT. Morning na picken of the sleep wey person sleep the night before, not so? Make we jus' lef am so. (*Busies herself with chores.*)

> Enter SANDA, *the Security Officer. He has a pile of magazines and a book under his arm.*

SANDA. Good morning, Mama Put!

MAMA PUT. How are you, my son?

SANDA. As you see, Mama, as you see. Morning, Mr Barber.

BARBER. Morning o, Security.

> TRADER *has dashed up the steps, righted the stool which was lying on its side, giving it a quick dusting.*

TRADER. You welcome, *oga*.

SANDA. Area Two-One!

TRADER. Na your hand we dey.

SANDA (*sees the* SHOP WORKER). Hey, you're early.

TRADER (*laughing*). 'In bobo trow am commot for house. Na here she sleep all night. E keep Judge warm for night.

SHOP WORKER. God punish your head! (*A car driving past is reflected in the sliding doors. The* SHOP WORKER *springs up.*) Manager done come.

SANDA (*looking up at the sky*). If this doesn't prove a hot day . . .

TRADER. Judge say na in dey make the climate now. E say na in dey tell the sky what to do. De man done craze *patapata*.

SANDA. Why? We do have professional rainmakers, don't we? What they claim to do is the same – tell the sky what to do.

TRADER. Oga self! *Haba*! No to different fancy dey take am every day? Only last week he tell us say 'e done sabbe how to make money. 'E swear say 'e go make all of us rich pass any drug baron.

SANDA. Well, give him time. Maybe he's still working on the magic formula.

TRADER. Wissai? I tell you say na weather and sunshine come interest am now. 'E done forget all about the money business.

SANDA. Genius, friend, genius. Great minds cannot rest content with only one idea at a time. And anyway, how do you know it's not all connected? If he wants to shower us with millions, he must first master the skies. Give him time. When it starts to rain millons, you won't have cause to complain.

TRADER (*amazed*). You tink is really possible, oga? You tink say 'e done find the secret?

SANDA (*taps his head*). Appearances are deceptive. There may be a method in his madness – that's what William Shakespeare says on the subject.

TRADER. Ah, that your friend again.

SANDA. Oh yes, he has an answer for everything.

> *The lights come on in the interior of the store. The door slides open and shut, as if being tested.* SANDA *takes his seat, and opens up one of his magazines.* BOYKO *practises a tune on his flute.*

BARBER. You know, Mr Sanda, to you it may seem a joke, but these things really happen you know.

SANDA. What things?

BARBER. Those who make money with black magic. I mean, there are people who do it. It is bad money. It doesn't always last, and the things people have to do to get such money, it's terrible business. Sometimes they have to sacrifice their near relations, even children. It's a pact with the devil but they do it.

SANDA. It's a pact with the devil all right, but it doesn't produce any money. They just slaughter those poor victims for nothing.

BARBER. Those overnight millionaires then, how do you think they do it?

SANDA. Cocaine. 419 swindle. Godfathering or mothering armed robbers. Or after a career with the police. Or the Army, if you're lucky to grab a political post. Then you retire at forty – as a General who has never fought a war. Or you start your own church, or mosque. That's getting more and more popular.

BARBER. You don't believe anything, that's your problem.

SANDA. There are far too many superstitions suffocating this country. I can't believe all of them, can I?

BARBER. This one is no superstition. Look, Trader, didn't I tell you about the landlord of my sister-in-law?

TRADER. Na true. Ah, oga, make you hear this one o. E take in eye see this one o, no to say den tell am.

SANDA. Don't bother. It's too early in the morning, my stomach won't be able to take it. (*To* BOYKO.) Fe. Fe. Not fa. When will you get that correct?

BARBER. You are the original doubting Thomas. But these things happen, that's all I can tell you. You see all those corpses with their vital organs missing – breasts in the case of women, the entire region of the vagina neatly scooped out. And sometimes just the pubic hair is shaved off for their devilish mixture. And pregnant ones with the foetus ripped out. Male corpses without their genitals or eyes. Sometimes they cut out the liver . . .

TRADER. And what of hunchbacks? Dat na another favourite for making money. They take out the hunch, sometimes while the man self still dey alive.

BARBER. Yes, that's supposed to be most effective, when the hunch is carved out with the owner still breathing. Some people have no hearts. They've sold their souls to the devil! Albinos too – don't forget them. Although I don't know what part of their body they use.

TRADER. No to the skin?

BARBER. No. Can't be. That one they picked up near Ita Faji cemetery had his birthday suit intact. He hadn't been skinned or anything like that. Even the eyes hadn't been touched. You would think it had something to do with the eyes – you know albinos don't like sunlight, maybe they drained the fluid from the eyes . . .

SANDA. Look, I've told you I don't want to hear all that kind of talk on an empty stomach. How soon will that *konkere* be ready, Mama Put?

MAMA PUT. Any time you people can take your minds off the satanic work of these get-rich-quick swine.

> *Enter* BLIND MINSTREL *with his box-guitar, singing 'Lagos is the place for me'. Stops when he reaches the food-stall. Greetings are exchanged and he fumbles in his pocket for money.* MAMA PUT *ladles out some bean pottage and fried stew.*

MAMA PUT. With or without?

MINSTREL (*brief hesitation*). With.

> *She sprinkles some* gari *over the pottage.*

SANDA. How are you this morning, Troubadour?

MINSTREL. As you see me, Bro., as you see me. Five naira *ewa* no fit fill picken belle these days, how much more grown man like me?

SANDA. A-ah. But the soldiers say life has improved since they took over.

MINSTREL. Perhaps for inside dere barracks. Not for my side of the street!

SANDA. Well, those who get, get. And they know how to spend it. Our banqueting-hall is booked for tonight. Plus the entire courtyard of the plaza. Big wedding ceremony. Broad Street is closed to traffic – from seven o'clock – all the way from the junction of Balogun Street to that flyover. Never happened before. The Military Governor himself signed the permit.

MINSTREL. Thank you, sir. I shall ensure my presence here in the evening.

SANDA. Don't even wait till then. Stay around the neighbourhood today. The relations will be coming and going all day, to oversee the arrangements. They are bound to be in a generous mood.

MINSTREL. I'll hang around then. Mama, I think I'll have some *sawa-sawa* with this *ewa* after all. Two naira. (*Flashing the money.*)

MAMA PUT. Keep counting your chickens before they're hatched.

MINSTREL. Mama Put, I can already hear the rustle of fat naira notes. My voice needs lubricating. So bring that other stuff you keep for special customers. Give me one shot with the change.

MAMA PUT. See what you've done? You've turned the poor beggar's head and he has not even earned the money he's spending. (*From the recesses of her cupboard, she brings out a bottle and pours him a shot.*) Here. Fortunately your voice can't be any more jarring than it is already.

SANDA. He'll earn it. There'll be plenty of bread to go round today. Even the prisoners won't be left out. A batch of them are already detailed to clean up the neighbourhood. They should get here in the afternoon. (*Chuckles.*) I suppose they'll expect me to give them an advance on their expectations.

MINSTREL (*gargles with the liquor and swallows. Beams*). We no go let you go back to your Rivers town, Mama Put. The way you sabbe brew this *kain-kain*, 'e no get competition for Lagos.

MAMA PUT (*brandishes what looks like a bayonet*). When I'm ready to move back, let's see who will try and stop me. (*Begins to cut up meat with the knife.*) It's bad enough that I've had to live in Lagos all these years; do you think I also want to die in it?

MINSTREL. You can't escape Lagos. Even for your Ikot Ekpene, you go find Lagos.

MAMA PUT. Yes, but not in such a strong dose. Lagos na overdose.

MINSTREL. True word, Mama Put, true word.

He laughs and plucks at his box-guitar. BOYKO, *as usual whenever there is any singing, manfully tries to accompany him.*

MINSTREL (*sings*).

I love dis Lagos, I no go lie
Na inside am I go live and die
I know my city, I no go lie
E fit in nation like coat and tie
When Lagos belch, the nations swell
When the nation shit, na Lagos dey smell.
The river wey flow for Makurdi market
You go find in deposit for Lagos bucket.

MAMA PUT. Hey, not that one near my food-stall, you hear?
MINSTREL. No blame me, blame Oga Sanda, na in teach me all the bad songs. Anyway, wait small. I nearly reach the part wey celebrate the Civil War wey drive you commot for Ikot Ekpene. I know na that part you like to hear. But first, make I salute we famous Lagosian landscape.

The Russian astronauts flying in space
Radioed a puzzle to their Moscow base
They said, we're flying over Nigeria
And we see high mountains in built-up area
Right in the middle of heavy traffic
Is this space madness, tell us quick?
The strange report was fed to computers
Which soon analysed the ponderous beauties
The computer replied, don't be snobbish
You know it's a load of their national rubbish.

They respond with laugher. Even MAMA PUT *allows herself a chuckle.*

But make I return to history
Dat war we fight in recent memory

When music wey come from barrel of gun
Was – we must keep the nation one.
Me I tink I get problem for me eye
I dey see double, thas the reason why
When I look, na two I see,
Make I explain, I tink you go gree.

MAMA PUT's *customers begin to drift in. They join in the
chorus: 'I love this Lagos'.*

Make you no worry, both nations be friends
When they fight, they soon make amends
When one back de itch, de other go scratch
One go lay eggs, de other go hatch
Eggs are eggs, and plenty done rotten
But make I tell you, some are golden
I tell you my country no be one
I mean, no to yesterday I born.
    I love this Lagos *etc.*

One twin go slap, the other go turn cheek
And soon they're playing Hide-and-Seek
Sixteen billion dollars or more
Wey be windfall from Saddam's war
Vanish for air like harmattan dust
Twin Seek cry, *Haba*, this country go bust
Brother Hide stay cool, he set up commission
Of enquiry with prompt decision
Seek from Turkey to China Sea
The more you look, the less you see.
    I love this Lagos *etc.*

The other day, I lie for my bed
And the radio suggest say I sick for my head
Cause the government say e get no option
But to wage war against corruption
I pinch myself to be sure I awake

Then I laugh so tey, my body ache
Pot tell calabash your belle de show
Snail tell tortoise, how come you so slow
Monkey go market, baboon dey cook
You tink one chop, de other siddon look?
Before battle start, the war done lost
Plus billions den go say the battle cost
   I love this Lagos *etc.*

Enter, during the singing a young GIRL, *in school uniform. She helps* MAMA PUT *in serving the customers, then spruces up to go to school, picks up her satchel.*

GIRL. Morning, Mr Sanda.

SANDA. Morning, sight for sore eyes. Now this boastful sunrise has some decent competition.

MAMA PUT (*gives her a quick once-over*). You have the new books? (*The* GIRL *pats her satchel.*) Don't lose them. It's all I can afford for now. Tell your teacher we'll get the rest next month. Or next term. Whenever God chooses to increase my profit. (*Hesitates. Looks up at* SANDA.) You know, I don't really want her to go to school today.

SANDA. Because of the missing textbooks? Come on.

MAMA PUT. No, it's that same dream . . . it came back again last night. I really think she should stay home today.

GIRL. Dreams can't take care of my schooling, Mama.

MAMA PUT. If I thought they could, I wouldn't be out here every morning sweating over these pots to pay for your school fees. And anyway, who was talking to you?

SANDA. Forget the bad dreams, Mama. Everyone has them from time to time. Believe it or not I dreamt only last week that I got married. But I still had to put on my uniform and come to work. All I wanted to do was to lock up the windows and doors, stuff up the cracks in the walls and hide under my bed.

MAMA PUT. Oh you! You make fun of everything. All right girl, off you go. Here, don't forget the money for your school lunch. And make sure you return here directly after school. Tell your teacher I don't want you on any after-school assignment. Not this week anyway.

GIRL. All right, Mother. Bye-bye Mr Sanda. (*She runs off.*)

SANDA (*shakes his head, smiling*). You really are some kind of Mother Courage, you know. Even right down to the super-stitious bit.

MAMA PUT. There are dreams and dreams. This one . . .

SANDA. . . . is exactly like the one you had before the last excite-ment on our street. What was it now? Oh yes, something terrible had happened to Lagos. You woke up one day and there wasn't any Lagos anywhere. No warning, no nothing, just – pouff! – Lagos was gone. Disappeared into thin air. And you thought that was a calamity!

MAMA PUT. Nobody cares to listen to me . . .

SANDA. You know we do. Someone has to do the worrying on the street after all, so we leave all that to you and carry on with normal life. It works perfectly, believe me.

MAMA PUT (*sighs. Stirs the pot, then looks up*). I don't remember waking up to a morning this bright. Not a blemish. There isn't even a speck of cloud in the sky.

SANDA. I'm glad you've noticed. Dark dreams at night, then daylight comes and banishes all the misgivings they sneak into the heart.

MAMA PUT. You are wrong, son. Woefully wrong. A sky such as this brings no good with it. The clouds have vanished from the sky but, where are they? (*Jabs the tip of the bayonet against her breast.*) In the hearts of those below. In the rafters. Over the hearth. Blighting the vegetable patch. Slinking through the orange grove. Rustling the plantain leaves and withering them – oh I heard them again last night – and poisoning the fish-pond. When the gods mean to be kind to us, they draw up the gloom to themselves – yes, a cloud is a good sign, only, not many people know that. Even a wisp, a mere shred of cloud over my roof would bring me comfort, but not this stark, cruel brightness. It's not natural. It's a deceit. You watch out. We'd better all watch out.

BOYKO looks upstage at some distraction, gets up and runs off.

SANDA (*softly*). You'll never get over that war. Not ever. Nobody does. It would be abnormal. But you must forget the fish-ponds, Mama. And the orange groves. This is Lagos, city of chrome and violence. Noise and stench. Lust and sterility. But it was here you chose to rebuild your life. You've done better than most, made a new home for your children. Sent them all to school and to university, just from frying and selling *akara* and concocting superlative bean pottage, not to mention the popular brew. You deserve a medal.

MAMA PUT. Medal! And what would I do with that? Keep your medals and give me back – yes, even the mangrove swamps. (*Sudden harshness. She waves the bayonet violently around.*) And don't remind me of medals! They all got medals. Those who did this thing to us, those who turned our fields of garden eggs and prize tomatoes into mush, pulp and putrid flesh – that's what they got – medals! They plundered the livestock, uprooted yams and cassava and what did they plant in their place? The warm bodies of our loved ones. My husband among them. My brothers. One of them they stabbed to death with this! And all for trying to save the family honour. Yes, and children too. Shells have no names on them. And the pilots didn't care where they dropped their bombs. But that proved only the beginning of the seven plagues. After the massacre of our youth came the plague of oil rigs and the new death of farmland, shrines and fish sanctuaries, and the eternal flares that turn night into day and blanket the land with globules of soot . . . I suppose those oilmen will also earn medals?

Enter BIG MAN SHOPPPER, pursued by BOYKO.

BIG MAN SHOPPER. Go away! I tell you I have no car for you to look after. Go and find yourself another customer.

BOYKO. Oga, this place no good. Anything can happen to your car. But if you lef' am to Boyko, na one hundred per cent guarantee.

BIG MAN SHOPPER (*stops and faces him squarely*). I think something is wrong with your ears.

BOYKO. Na all this traffic noise, oga, 'e fit make man so deaf 'e no go hear en'ting, even thunder self. Even if dem dey break windscreen for Mercedes in broad daylight for in very front, person no fit hear.

BIG MAN SHOPPER. Is that so?

BOYKO. To God who made me!

BIG MAN SHOPPER. Well, young man, you'd better pray for a miracle from the same God who made you so you can hear me when I say (*Bellows.*) Get off me! Scram! I have no Mercedes whose windscreen you and your gang can break.

> *He breaks off and walks down briskly, turns the corner and mounts the steps. The boy slouches after him.*

SANDA (*looks up lazily from his journal*). Has that boy been annoying you, sir?

BIG MAN SHOPPER. Don't mind him. He thinks people aren't wise to their tricks. I no longer park where vandals and extortionists like him operate.

SANDA. Very sensible. That space just under the flyover – where the fish trucks supply the market women – that's one of the safest places. I always recommend it. Nothing can touch your car there.

BIG MAN SHOPPER. Oh no, it's much better behind the old UAC building. The gang doesn't operate in that area at all; it's too close to the military pay office.

SANDA. You're right. They daren't mess about near those soldiers. Enjoy your shopping, sir.

> BIG MAN SHOPPER *enters the store.* SANDA *resumes his reading.* BOYKO *remains near* TRADER's *stall, below* SANDA, *who*

has picked up another journal and appears to be checking a list within it. He speaks without taking his face off the magazine.

Yeah. Just wanted to make sure, but it's the same old Toyota Crown, at least when owner was last registered. (*Runs his finger down the journal.*) LA 6161 OD – Tell Area Two-Four to take care of it, then return here so you can take him warning when our Big Man has finished his shopping. (BOYKO *sets off.*) Wait! Warn Two-Four he shouldn't be fooled by the car's ancient appearance – it's brand-new inside. Tell him to tackle the boot – that's where he keeps his briefcase. If it's not there, take the radio and the seat-covers – it's all high-class stuff. Go!

BOYKO *runs off.* SANDA *sighs, shakes his head dolefully. He speaks as if to no one in particular.*

If there's one thing I hate, it's disloyality. People should be loyal. We used to look after that man, never any complaint. If he wished, he could leave all the doors of his car open and there'd be nothing missing on his return. Heaven knows what gets into all of them these days. All kinds of duplicity from those who should set an example. Why dent the sides of a custom-built Toyota, just to make it look like a botched-up panel-beater job. And then the paint! Looks more like surface primer blended with rust. But just you take a look inside – drinks cabinet, a dainty little refrigerator – very cute – I wouldn't mind something like that myself, only, where does it go on a motorbike? The chamois leather seats – well now, a strip of that will have no problem on the seat of the motorbike. No, the interior of that car is something else – polished oak panelling on the doors, electronic dashboard, rugs so deep your feet don't notice the pot-holes. You'd never suspect any of that. You'll walk past that beat-up Toyota, wondering why such junk should be licensed to ply the motor road. But we got the inside picture all right. (*Chuckles.*) Two-One!

TRADER. I dey here, oga.

SANDA. I say do you remember that camouflage man?

TRADER. No to him pass enter shop just now? We no see am since last year riot.

SANDA. Yeah. If he had not taken one of our – er – pilots on board, for safe passage, we'd never have known what the interior of his Toyota really looked like.

TRADER. The pilot charge him double after he see all dat super fancy interior. In fact, I remember, he even wan' cancel his safe conduct altogether.

SANDA. No, we couldn't allow that. A deal is a deal. (*Sighs.*) We had such a nice community here – we still do. Once you're registered, that's it for life. Now he goes and hides his car outside our area. It hurts one's pride. (*Shakes his head reprovingly.*) People should support their community. (*He resumes his reading.*)

TRADER. True talk. Even oyinbo man 'in say, charity begin for home.

> A CYCLIST *has slowed down in front of his stall.* TRADER *appears mesmerised by this visitation. The* CYCLIST *inspects the goods, but* TRADER's *attention is focused entirely on the bicycle.*

CYCLIST. How much this tie, oga?

TRADER. Oga Sanda, you see wetin I take my eye see?

CYCLIST. What? I say this tie. Wetin be last price?

> TRADER *gets up slowly, as if in a trance. He circles the bicycle, warily.*

TRADER. Oga Sanda, make you look this ting wey I dey look so o. Mama Put, Mr Barber, all of una, make you come look o. Because I no believe this thing at all at all, even though my eye tell me say no to dream I dey dream am.

NEWSVENDOR (*enters, pressing his bullhorn*). City News. Daily

Courier. National . . . (*Stops dead, transfixed in turn by the contraption.*) Sho!

BARBER (*also approaching. Looks from the bicycle to the* CYCLIST). Maybe there is a circus in town.

NEWSVENDOR. No, no news of circus for any of my newspaper.

MAMA PUT. I feel homesick. Oh, the sight of this thing, it makes me feel homesick.

TRADER. But you mean say na true? Na true true this machine here, or na magic?

CYCLIST. Wes matter with all of una? I say I wan' price this tie.

BARBER. Was he the one? Did you bring this contraption here?

CYCLIST. Wetin be contraption? Why you all dey take eye look me as if to say I be one *saka-jojo*?

MAMA PUT. It makes me homesick, that's all I can say. It just makes me feel so homesick I want to pack up and go home. Today. (*Returns to her corner.*)

NEWSVENDOR. Wey all these reporters self? Man no dey see them when something extra dey happen. O-oh, if to say I just get camera.

CYCLIST (*bristling*). Camera! For what? I be freak show? I get two head or you see tail commot from my yansh? Look, if you try . . . !

BARBER. No, no, please. Please don't take offence. We are all naturally curious, you see. Did you actually bring this thing into town. I mean, ride it into town?

CYCLIST. How you think say I get here? Of course na ride I ride am. All the way from new Ajegunle settlement. You wan' make I carry am instead?

TRADER. I fit touch am? You no go vex? I just wan' touch am small.

NEWSVENDOR. Me too.

CYCLIST. Wetin come dey worry all you people? All this *wahala* just beause I wan' buy tie? Na trade you come trade or na decorate you just dey decorate street?

BARBER. You know, if a submarine were to surface here, it could not cause a greater sensation. Even a spaceship from outer space.

That reminds me, Mr Sanda, I have still to take you to that preacher who was abducted by spacemen in their flying saucer . . .

SANDA. Sure, sure . . .

BARBER. Seven months and seven days he spent with them. They landed the saucer in his front garden you know. All silver and blue, about the size of a football field . . .

SANDA. And it landed in his front garden.

BARBER. It could contract and expand, like an accordion. It expanded to its full size as it took off . . .

CYCLIST (*drops the tie*). All of una, I tink you dey take me play. I go take my business go somewhere else.

SANDA. You don't understand, my friend. Even I, I don't recall when I last I saw one of those in the streets of Lagos. It is quite a sight, I promise.

TRADER. I tell you this na wonderful. Wonderful! A real bicycle inside Lagos. Which place you find am?

BARBER. He must be part of a circus. You know, those cycling acrobats. The Chinese were at the National Theatre last week, remember?

SANDA. Don't be daft. Does he look Chinese to you?

BARBER. They did magic too, you forget, very good magic. Disappearing and cutting themselves in two and so on. You think they can't turn themselves into Lagosians like you and me?

SANDA. Your mind and magic and all kinds of superstition! Where are you from, my friend?

CYCLIST. Ajegunle new settlement. And na tie I wan buy, that's all. But e be say dat one done become commotion. Who get this stall? E wan' sell tie abi 'e no dey sell?

TRADER (*rushing back behind his stall*). Ah, sorry, sorry. I sorry too much. No vex, my friend. Na de ting wey bring you come cause all the wonderment. Wetin you wan' buy? Take your time, I beg. Everyting na reduce price, specially for you. You go see, I go give you special reduction. (*His attention is still partially on the bicycle.*) You say you like the tie? How much you wan' pay? Ah, but this is wonderful. The last time I see bicycle for this Lagos na before the oil boom. Enh? You mean to say somebody still dey, wey no troway in bicycle inside lagoon? (*Rakes down a whole row of ties and hands them over.*) Make you look am proper. Choose the one wey fit gentleman like yourself. (*Sneaks back to the bicycle. Spins the pedals.*) No vex for me o, I just wan' . . . (*Rings the bell. Rings it again, delightedly.*) Na original oga. Na genuine pedal locomotion, the kind my great, great grandpa dem call iron horse when oyinbo missionary first ride one for Lagos last century. (*Looks wistfully at* CYCLIST.) You no mind, my friend? I just wan' see if I still fit balance.

CYCLIST (*gives up*). Do anything wey you want. Make you no wreck am, thas all. Because na borrow I borrow am.

NEWSVENDOR. Me too, my brother. Make I ride am small, I beg. Ha, if to say I be reporter, na scoop of the year 'e for be. If only man fit get photographer . . .

TRADER. Na waya for me today. (*Jumps on it and rides, barely able to balance.*) Common bicycle. Inside this very Lagos of oil-boom and daily millionaire. I tink say everyone done smash in bicycle or sell 'am for scrap iron.

CYCLIST (*trying on the ties*). You wait small. As our people say, na cudgel go teach crazeman sense; na hunger go reform labourer picken wey dream say in papa be millionaire. When the time come, na *omolanke*, common push-cart, na 'in even senior service go take go work. Na *omolanke* go full expressway inself.

TRADER (*chuckling as he wobbles from side to side*). True word, my brother. Before before, for early morning, na bicycle dey jam-pack Carter Bridge as people dey ride go begin work or return go home. Den, oil boom come. Government dash everybody salary increase, salary advance, salary arrears, motor car advance, motor car incentive, motorcycle advance, all kind vehicle allowance, any kind incentive.

CYCLIST. My friend, make we forget better time. No to that time de Minister of Finance inself boast for budget speech say, any increment wey no dey, we go increment am?

TRADER. Any allowance wey no dey, we go allow. (*Both burst into laughter*.)

BARBER (*from across*). No forget the other one – any incentive wey no dey for worker, we go incent! (*They roar with laughter*.)

CYCLIST. That man make the whole country tink say money just dey fall from sky.

TRADER. Why not? Wetin you wan' make common Minister make 'e say when in own Head of State done announce to the world dat – de problem we get for de nation no be money, but how to spend 'am. Abi na my memory dey lie?

CYCLIST (*reproachful annoyance*). Oh look, why you come now dey remember better time? E be like say man wey go sleep wit' empty belle come begin dream say 'e dey inside wedding feast. When 'e wake up, in suffer-suffer go double.

> MINSTREL *begins the song: 'Alaaru T'o Nje Buredi'. Gets up after a verse or two, crosses the stage, still singing, his voice remaining audible in the neighbourhood for some time. The* NEWSVENDOR *takes over the bicycle for a while.*

TRADER. No mind me, I beg. Na this sight of your bicycle come begin remind me. Sai! Dat time, money dey walka street and buka, supermarket and corner shop like 'e no get tomorrow. Everybody just dey blow money as if Father Christmas siddon inside aeroplane, begin scatter manna from heaven . . . Even schoolchildren, 'e be like say den begin shit money.

SANDA. Do you never tire of all that good-old-days belly-aching? My friend, pay no attention to him. Tell him to migrate to the Republic of China where everybody rides bicycles. Then ask him if he himself didn't profiteer plenty from that Udoji oil bonanza.

TRADER. If not why not? I be trader, not so? I think say market be like prostitute – money for hand, open ya leg. I sell stereo . . . everything from video to electric toothbrush. Automatic become de national craze – because why? Because nobody wan use in own power again. But time done change. Austerity done catch monkey. Ah, na special tie dat one o, my customer.

CYCLIST. Hn-hn. How much?

TRADER. Ninety naira, my brother, and only because you be my first customer.

CYCLIST. Ninety nai . . . ! *Haba*, my friend, oil boom done finish now.

TRADER. But devaluation never stop. Remember say ninety naira today na only one dollar. So, make you tell me, you fit buy that kin' tie for America for one dollar? Na dat kind eye make you take look am. Look the label . . . look am, look am . . . Made in Florida, USA. You tink na one dollar 'e cost for USA?

CYCLIST. Even so . . .

TRADER. Na first-class tie. Proper bargain. If to say we government dey give American people visa as dem dey want am, na for dis very place Americans go come do them shopping. Den own goods cheap here pass the very place where den dey manufacture am.

CYCLIST. You sure say dis no to Made in Taiwan?

TRADER. Look label now. You tink say na me put label dere?

CYCLIST. But you sabbe say those Taiwanese can put Made in Paris, or London, even Made on the Moon for anything they make for dem backyard.

TRADER. Come on my friend. I can see say you no sabbe trade at all. Taiwanese no dey bring ties here, na only motor spare part. If na spare parts you talk, en-hen, I no go argue with you, but as for ties . . . Believe me, Made in Florida na Made in USA – make we no waste any more time. Eighty naira – dat na my very last price. You fit go try somewhere else if you no believe me.

> CYCLIST *takes one more look at the effect of the tie against his shirt, using one of the small mirrors also on sale. He nods. Begins to give it a fat knot around his neck. Then moves on to the sunglasses, trying them on, one after the other.* BOYKO *returns, squats down by* TRADER's *stall.*

CYCLIST. OK. You catch me cheap cheap because I get appointment with one sisi for later. Na in make I go borrow my brother's bicycle self because man no fit trust public transport again. You wait for bus all day and then, when one *molue* finally arrive enh, then Somalia war go begin. Shirt and trouser wey you done wash and iron to blow employer mind or scatter girlfriend in sense – (*Hisses.*) – e become like rag for second-hand *bosikona* market . . .

TRADER. Oh, na me you dey tell tory? Na drama for that bus-stop – (*Points.*) – every day, every morning going for work or evening time after work. Everyone for inself, man or woman, old or young – nobody care. One third body inside, one leg outside, remainder under luggage and other people's body. I done see big man – e fat plenty – dem squeeze am so hard, 'e shit inside in trousers.

CYCLIST. Ugh! I beg, make we talk better ting for early morning time. (*He appears to have made up his mind about the glasses, a psychedelic styled model.*) This one, how much?

TRADER. Take am one-twenty last. Honest, me I no dey like haggle for early morning.

CYCLIST. Hundred.

TRADER (*heatedly*). Look, you no hear me talk say . . . ?

CYCLIST. Hundred. Is all for this interview wey I get tomorrow, and na my brother borrow me de money. Na two thing I dey buy from you now. Haba, you no go give me special discount? Even for sake of good luck for my interview. If I get the job, you go know say na you help me.

TRADER (*makes as if outraged, then simmers down*). All right. Put five on top hundred – for sake of good luck. And after all, you give me my bicycle ride for first time in twenty years.

CYCLIST (*beams with satisfaction as he takes out the money*). Tomorrow na tomorrow. Since all dis time wey I dey write application – more than two hundred application for three years, no only now den give me chance for interview.

SANDA. If you don't get the job, ride your bicycle this way again. Sometimes, I get to know about vacancies you know – all the big people who come here, when they need driver or steward or this and that, they come and ask me to help them.

CYCLIST. God bless you, sir. God bless una both.

He jumps on his bicycle. Before he is even balanced however, the BARBER *clicks his clippers at him and points to the placard displaying his range of styles. The* CYCLIST *hesitates.*

BARBER. For that interview, I would recommend the Lumumba Slide-Back.

CYCLIST. I don't have the time.

BARBER. Your interview is not till tomorrow.

CYCLIST. Yes, but right now, I have an appointment with one . . .

BARBER. I heard. The more reason to knock her out with a brand-new haircut. Don't worry, I don't waste time. And it's fifty per cent discount since you are my first customer.

CYCLIST (*attracted by the model on the placard*). You really think . . . ?

BARBER. Definitely the Lumumba Slide-Back for you. It would clinch the job. And the girl.

CYCLIST *gets down and begins to prop up his bicycle.*

CYCLIST. All right. If you're sure it won't take long.

BARBER. I am known for my lightning clippers. Even the soldiers know me. I can shave the head of an entire batallion between one coup and the next. Sit down and relax your back. Cycling is not easy when you've abandoned it for some time. I made that mistake once, many years ago. I couldn't get up for days afterwards.

TRADER (*rushes to relieve him of the bicycle*). Make a warm am for you while Barber dey do your hair.

BARBER. Warm what up? It hasn't got an engine. (*Starts preparing his client for the haircut.*)

TRADER. You know sabbe anything about bicycle. If the pedal get too cold, the wheel no go turn properly. Even handle, 'e go become stiff. (*Rides off.*)

BARBER. All the street mongrels are going to snap at your heels, you'll see. Area Boy on bicycle! The police will use it as an excuse to lock you up, mark my words. Mr Sanda, you'd better get ready to go and bail him.

SANDA. It's a free country.

BARBER. Is it? I'm sure this fellow got so far on his machine because people were taken by surprise. And he is a stranger around here. Otherwise, it could easily have caused a riot.

TRADER (*rides in, singing*).

I thought it was a case of an optical illusion
I don't recall a journey in a time-machine
Damn it! This is Lagos, not a rural seclusion
And nineteen ninety-four, far from colonial mission
No one worth his mettle goes pedalling a bike
Not even with petroleum on an astronomic hike
There's something fishy here, or else a miracle
To see a Lagos body on a bicycle
Chorus:
There's something fishy here, or else a miracle
   To see a Lagos body on a bicycle

Rides off again during the chorus.

BARBER.

The city's gone to pieces if this can really happen
They're trying to pull us back to some prehistoric age
Evil is on the loose; we've got our wits to sharpen
Supernatural forces are out to dent our image
Not even children ride a bike to school – it's indecent
It shames the home, embarrasses the status-conscious parent
Even a messenger would go on strike for an official vehicle
Than be caught dead delivering letters on a bicycle.
   Even a messenger *etc.*

MAMA PUT.

Once the palm-wine tapper's trade was a performance test
How he kept his balance was a sight for jaded eyes

With frothing gourds on either side, his cradle round his chest
The cycle was his camel, a most practical device
For navigating bush paths, then rolling into town
To quench the burning fire of thirst beneath the worker's
                                                    frown
But now the tapper thinks himself a butt of ridicule
To enter the big city on a bicycle.
 But now the tapper *etc.*

SANDA.
A motorcycle is the lowest Lagos can accomodate
And preferably nothing less than a five-hundred c.c.
State of the art, aerodynamic, not a detail out of date
With a fierce accelerating roar, or else you're just a cissy.
But the car is really it – Japan, US or Scandinavia
Before it's unveiled at source, it's cruising in Nigeria
Transfer of technology? We've passed that obstacle.
It's Benz, Rolls-Royce or Lexus – don't prescribe a bicycle!
 Transfer of technology *etc.*

BARBER.
Oh, a sight like this is a portent to be exorcised
The devil's at his dirty work, it's pure satanism
We've private gyms if flabby muscles must be exercised
And jogging's the in-thing for those free of rheumatism
So the roads are pot-holed, and public transportation
Dead? There's foreign exchange for private car importation.
This is boom-town, where heretics of the Mammon oracle
Are run out frontier-style, tied backwards to a bicycle.
 This is boom-town *etc.*

Re-enter the BIG MAN SHOPPER.

SANDA. Would you like me to get you some help for that, sir?
 Where are all these small boys . . . ?
BIG MAN SHOPPER. No thank you. That's how the no-good vandals

get to know where one parks his car. I can manage by myself.
Much safer that way.

SANDA. Very sensible, sir, very sensible.

The MINSTREL's *song has changed to: 'Adelebo T'o Nwoko'.*
The song weaves in and out of hearing until the entry of
MISEYI.

The NEWSVENDOR *accosts* BIG MAN SHOPPER *as he reaches*
street level, following him into the alleyway.

NEWSVENDOR. *Business Times*, Sir? Or *City Gent*? I get latest
Expose and *Newswrite*. Comrade Ugo Bassa done explode for
Update! Sensational interview, sir, sensational! Look am sah,
make you just look de cover. Den say Minister of Commerce
may resign because of drug scandal. Only twenty-five naira!
Copies nearly finish. (*Switches to a low singsong voice, as he*
quickly dips in a pouch and fishes out a different batch of
magazines and video casettes.) Hot, hot, hot . . . Adult magazines sir . . . Hot, hot, hot . . . Sexy videos . . . Hot, hot, hot . . .
Secret Nights in the Bishop's Vestry . . . Hot, hot, hot . . .
Madonna Meets the Prince of Darkness – Sai! – Sizzling hot, hot,
hot – the very latest, not yet officially released . . . Sex Slaves in
Saudi Arabia – Hot, hot, hot – na we own pilgrims just smuggle
am commot for Jeddah. You not fit get copy anywhere else . . .

BIG MAN SHOPPER. Will you take your dirty merchandise elsewhere
before I set the police on you?

NEWSVENDOR. Sorry sir, make you no vex. But I also get the latest
releases from Hollywood. Even self, dey no release them yet for
anywhere. I get *Terminator IV* and *V* – half price. And all the
films wey den nominate for Oscar, everything reach here even
before the Oscar and Academy people begin see the film . . .

Disappears with him through the rear.

BARBER. . . . with these my very eyes, I tell you, with these my very
eyes. I went to visit them one day, you know, the sister-in-law I
was telling you about. Their landlord was this chief, he lived

upstairs in his own apartment, all by himself. Apartment? More like a palace.

CYCLIST. Oh yes, I sabbe de kind. Na penthouse den dey call am. Proper luxury.

BARBER. Wait till you see this one. It had a covered roof garden into the bargain. And that roof garden had a small hut in a corner. So – here, take the mirror. How does that look from this side? Shall I take a little bit more off? It's my own original variation on the popular Lumumba cut, but you can tell me how you yourself want it.

CYCLIST. It's er . . . yes, it's fine on that side. Go on with your story.

BARBER. Ay yes. You won't believe it but . . . anyway, the husband said, let's go and pay a courtesy visit to the Chief . . .

CYCLIST. The landlord?

BARBER. Thank you, the landlord. Let's go and visit the landlord, he said, he always likes to meet my relations. So, up we went. Did I tell you it was evening, quite dark?

CYCLIST. You had finished dinner, you said.

BARBER. And finished watching the nine o'clock news. I was about to take my leave in fact but my in-law said, let's go and say Hallo to the Chief. So, up we went. But you know what? We couldn't find the Chief. The door was open, we went in, we called out several times, but there was no answer from the Chief. Shall I trim it all the way down to the neckline?

CYCLIST. Yes, yes, go on.

BARBER. I told you this wouldn't take long. It's all practice, you know. I can do almost any style even while sleeping.

CYCLIST. The landlord, where was he?

BARBER. I told you, there was no sign of him. So, my in-law said, well, I shall tell him we did call on him. And we decided to turn back. That was the moment we first heard the noise.

TRADER (dissatisfied with listening from a distance, he has been moving steadily nearer). Tell him what kin' noise. No forget that detail.

BARBER. A choking noise.

CYCLIST. Someone was trying to choke him?

BARBER. No, not that kind of choking. I can't really describe it. As if someone was vomiting and cursing at the same time. That kind of choking. We rushed there, thinking the Chief might be in pain or was taken ill, might even be dying. That's what we were thinking. So we rushed to the room but the door was locked. What to do? It was my in-law who noticed that the window was opened, so we rushed there – that was when we saw what we saw.

CYCLIST. What? What?

BARBER. Keep still, my friend. I don't want anyone to accuse my hands of being unsteady.

TRADER. You can't blame him. Didn't I nearly fall into the gutter myself when you first told me what happened?

CYCLIST. Well, go on. What happened? What did you see?

BARBER. A human head! No, before that, we saw the landlord. He was lying face down naked, prostrated on the floor, stark-naked I tell you. Not a piece of cloth on him.

CYCLIST. Stark-naked? And the head. What about the head?

BARBER. Ah yes, that was on a white table – no, I lie – a table covered in white cloth, like an altar, covered all the way to the ground. And that human head was sitting on the table, yes, sitting squarely on its neck, neatly sliced off – here!

CYCLIST (*flinches as the* BARBER *draws a finger across his neck*). Oh my god! Was it freshly cut?

BARBER. Not a drop of blood. But . . .

TRADER. Now you'll hear it for yourself. My oga doesn't believe in it but you'll hear it for yourself.

BARBER. A book was opened in front of the head . . .

CYCLIST. Hen? You mean that head dey read?

BARBER. The book was open, that's all I say. I never claim beyond what my eyes clearly saw. The book – was – open. My in-law says it must have been the Sixth and Seventh Book of Moses, you know, the missing ones, well known for conjuring. But we didn't enter. I didn't have the courage to enter and check for myself.

Who wants to run mad seeing what human eyes are not meant to see?

CYCLIST. So then what? The head, what about the head?

BARBER. The mouth of that head was wide open, just like the eyes. And it was vomiting – notes! Crisp naira notes. Fifty-naira denomination.

CYCLIST. Na so! Na so den dey do 'am. Na so my brother tell me before.

BARBER. In neat bundles. With the paper band around each neat package. As if it was coming straight from Central Bank.

TRADER. Na from dere. Na from dere 'e take magic conjurate am fly commot.

BARBER. Or the mint itself.

TRADER. Or the mint.

SANDA. Or your head, you foolish barber. You think I haven't been listening?

BARBER. You listen but you don't learn. Look, my friend, don't you mind that unbeliever. I saw it with my very eyes. The whole floor was covered, nearly up to the window level. That landlord was already buried in it – in fact, we just managed to see him.

SANDA. I thought you saw him stark naked from top to toe.

BARBER (*heatedly*). With all that money pouring down in bundles and falling off his body, anyone could see he was stark-naked.

SANDA. And to think you all say the Judge is mad. If your story is not rank lunacy on the loose . . .

> A FOREIGNER *moves onto the frontage from the direction of the parking lot, accompanied by the* PARKING ATTENDANT, *with whom he is arguing furiously.*

FOREIGNER. I already paid once. I'm damned if I'm going to pay a second time.

PARKING ATTENDANT. Then show me your receipt, sir. It's very simple what I'm asking – your receipt.

FOREIGNER. And I keep telling you I was not given one. I do not have a receipt to show you.

PARKING ATTENDANT. In that case, sir, you cannot leave your car in the parking lot. You must return and remove it at once.

FOREIGNER. What sort of a swindle is this? It's a bloody racket and you're all in on it. I'm damned if I let you play me for a sucker.

PARKING ATTENDANT. You can't leave your car in the car park without paying, those are the rules. I have the receipt book here – in your own interest, pay me, sir. If you don't, your car will be towed by the time you return.

SANDA. Is there some problem? Can I be of help, sir?

FOREIGNER (*suspiciously*). Who are you?

SANDA. Store Security personnel, sir. Maybe I can help.

FOREIGNER. I hope you can, my friend, because I'm getting damned near tired of being ripped off everywhere I go in this damned country. I pay to have my car garaged . . .

PARKING ATTENDANT. Which kin' pay? Show me your receipt.

SANDA. Let the man talk. You'll have your turn in a moment.

FOREIGNER. Thank you, sir. But look, let me first ask you, is that parking lot over there not an official one?

SANDA. It is, sir.

FOREIGNER. Good. Now, do you have more than one set of people collecting parking fees?

SANDA. A-ah, I see what the problem is. Yes, yes, I think I can see what happened. You must have fallen into the hands of the Insurance people.

FOREIGNER. Insurance? It's a hired car. Fully insured.

SANDA. No, I'm afraid you don't understand. Er, let me see, were you offered a choice at all?

FOREIGNER. A choice of what? What are you talking about?

SANDA. Ah, of course not, I forgot. You being a foreigner, you'd probably just have been charged the standard rate. How much did you pay?

FOREIGNER. Seven naira fifty. They asked for ten, but I beat it down. I'm only three months old in the country but I'm not totally green you know. I'm quite dry behind the ears – I haggled and beat them down to seven naira fifty kobo.

SANDA. Hm. You were given the discounted rate for foreigners. Normally it's ten naira for comprehensive insurance, five for third party.

FOREIGNER. Sorry, I don't think I get you. Are we talking about the same thing?

SANDA. Well, you do know what insurance is, I expect. The same principle operates with these . . . oh, it's embarrassing, I mean . . . you're right, it's extortion but, I'm afraid that's what goes on here. Everybody puts up with it, and the police condone it.

FOREIGNER. Could you explain please? I haven't quite caught on.

SANDA. I am sorry; I thought it would be quite clear by now. Comprehensive is always advisable because, then, the safety of your car is absolutely guaranteed. You see, sometimes, you have more than one gang operating. So, if you took Third Party, it exposes you to third party risks. Another gang could come and 'do' your car, and you see, the first gang wouldn't interfere. It's the code they have among themselves. Once a gang leaves a sign on your car which says 'Comprehensive', that's it. All other gangs keep off. Third Party buys you immunity only from the party to whom you paid.

FOREIGNER. I . . . I'm trying not to understand what you're telling me.

PARKING ATTENDANT (*disgustedly*). What is there left to understand? The man has taken the trouble to explain to you that you've paid your money to the wrong people. (*Laughs.*) And you don't even know if you have comprehensive or third party . . .

SANDA. Oh no, I'm sure it's comprehensive. They must have been teasing you with that haggling act – that was all pretence. The seven naira fifty is the foreigner's special rate – I hear them discussing these things all the time, though I pretend not to listen.

FOREIGNER. This is outrageous. How come they're allowed to get away with it?

PARKING ATTENDANT. The police station is over there – go and report if you like. But if I leave here without collecting your parking fee and giving you a receipt, I'm sending for a towing vehicle. Two naira fifty please, if you'll be so obliging.

FOREIGNER. You know what this bloody well does, don't you. It gives a very bad impression of you people to foreigners. You're driving people away from your country. Airport, the same grab. Customs ditto. Dash, kola, bread, wetin-you-carry, donation, gift, sweet-belle . . . I love that one – oga, make you pass me some sweet-belle now – very poetic – I thought I had mastered all the extortion rackets going on – two dozen at least – and now you tell me there's another one called Insurance.

TRADER. Wetin dis man dey talk about? You no get protection racket for your country? Abi no to your Europe dem place, and America dey come perfect protection and Mafia and wetin else? De Nigerians wey dem kill for America dis last year alone, e pass twelve, all because they refuse pay protection money. Some na simple taxi driver, one wey dem report for paper only last week, 'e just dey push ice-cream bicycle. Den shoot am to death because 'e refuse to pay . . .

SANDA. Pay no attention to my friend. He's a firebrand. He is planning to go into politics. Very nationalist. But he's right, you know . . .

FOREIGNER (weakly). It's the principle of the thing . . .

TRADER. Which kin' principle? You fall victim to common *wayo* people, and you begin cry like woman. For your country, if you make correct payment, you no go ask for receipt? Commot my friend!

SANDA (at his smoothest). Now, now, that's not the way to speak to our foreign guests. The man has had a bad experience, and it should make us feel ashamed. Our visitors should feel protected. I tell you what, sir, you leave the park attendant and me to sort this out . . .

FOREIGNER. No, no, it's all right. I'll pay.

SANDA. No, sir, I insist. I apologise for my countrymen. Please, go in and enjoy your shopping. I'll settle with the attendant and he will personally see that your car is given full protection.

FOREIGNER. I really hate to . . .

SANDA. It's perfectly all right, sir. I'm sure you would do the same for me if I happened to be in your country and the same thing happened to me. I'll get you a small boy to help you carry your purchases when you've finished.

FOREIGNER (*going*). This is really most decent of you, I must say . . . (*Enters shop.*)

> BIG MAN SHOPPER *erupts from the rear end of the alleyway, his fingers firmly attached to* BOYKO's *ear as he drags him along.*

BIG MAN SHOPPER. You don't fool me one bit. You're part of the gang and I am taking you to the police. When they give you the proper treatment you'll confess who your real bosses are. An honest, hardworking citizen can't even go about his normal business, thanks to street garbage like you. You think I don't know you're the lookout? That's the way you all begin and you end up armed robbers . . .

> SANDA *casts one brief look at them as they come round the corner, calmly puts his book down and awaits them.*

SANDA. What's the matter, sir? Can I help?

BIG MAN SHOPPER. Oh yes, Security, I've got one of them. They burglarised my car. They broke into the boot and stole my briefcase, tore out the radio . . .

SANDA. Impossible! In our parking lot?

BIG MAN SHOPPER. No, it was parked . . . I told you where it was parked. This young robber must have been watching me. He didn't fool me with his eye-service, dashing towards me and offering to carry my shopping. He was coming straight from where my Toyota was parked. I saw him.

BOYKO. That's what he keeps saying. Just because I see a big man and I go and help him carry his bags. He doesn't want to give me a tip, that's all.

BIG MAN SHOPPER. Shut up! You're one of them. Your gang vandalised my car and took my briefcase.

BOYKO. If you don't want to tip me, just say so. Don't use the problem of your car as an excuse. A big man like you, trying to cheat a small boy . . .

SANDA. Quiet! Don't mind him, sir. Honestly, I don't know what kind of children the country is producing these days. Someone old enough to be your father is talking and you keep putting your mouth in his. Don't mind him, sir.

BIG MAN SHOPPER. I'll teach him manners today – at the police station. Just take care of him for me while I get the police. In fact, I should have taken him to the Army barracks and let the soldiers deal with him.

SANDA. The Army, sir? Sure, they might give him some lashes and lock him in their guardroom but, they don't run things around here. They themselves find it convenient – sometimes – to pay protection money. After all, they understand what it's all about – that's why they keep seizing power. They're past masters of extortion – oh, pay me no attention, I get carried away sometimes. Now let's see. The problem is that place where you parked – it is actually outside our supermarket area. I can't very well lock him up in our detention room . . .

BIG MAN SHOPPER. Please, don't create unnecessary problems. Security is security. Lock him in your toilet if you like. If we don't keep him we'll never catch the rest of the gang.

SANDA. Well, sir, you know. Management is very careful about this sort of thing. If it had taken place within our jurisdiction, you understand, by now we would know what to do. But to involve Management, especially if it turns out that we've gone and locked up an innocent boy . . .

BIG MAN SHOPPER. Innocent! Are you telling me he's innocent when I tell you I saw him coming from the car. He was beside the car, then he started racing towards me, doing eye-service. There was a man at the same time . . .

SANDA (*turns fiercely on the boy*). Aha, what have you to say to that? Did you or did you not have an accomplice.

A crowd begins to gather.

BOYKO. Nobody, I never see anybody. Just the normal people coming and going.

BIG MAN SHOPPER. Let's get him to a police station. That's the only answer.

SANDA. Wait, sir. I have an idea. (*Turns to the* TRADER.) My friend, I beg, come.

TRADER. Me? Ah, who will look after my stall?

SANDA (*fakes impatience*). Come, my friend! Which kin' stall? No to me dey look after 'am when you go chop or follow woman? Come! As for all you people, scram! Go about your business. Who invited you come watch cinema show? Mr Trader . . .

TRADER. All right, all right. I dey come. E just be like man no fit trust anyone any more these days. Imagine small boy like this . . .

SANDA. Keep your eye on this rascal for me while I have a word with oga here. He's a regular customer, even though we haven't seen him for some time. But you know, once a neighbourhood member, always a member. We must do our bit for him. The matter is actually outside my jurisdiction but . . . Come, sir. I have an idea. (*He takes* BIG MAN SHOPPER *aside.*) Yes, sir, you are right, we could go to the police.

BIG MAN SHOPPER. Let's do that rightaway. We've lost too much time already.

SANDA. But then again, sir, you know what the police are like. (BIG MAN SHOPPER *becomes instantly crestfallen.*) Yes, sir, I am glad to see you do. He's only small fry, and his real bosses will simply come and bail him out, and that's the last you will see of him, and your missing valuables. The police will take their money and forget you.

BIG MAN SHOPPER (*sighs*). I have documents in that suitcase. Even my passport. The money doesn't matter so much, but I have important business papers . . .

SANDA. That's the way it usually goes. Now, I don't have to tell you, in this job, one must have one's ear to the ground, know all kinds of people.

BIG MAN SHOPPER (*sudden optimism*). You think you may be able to . . . pass the word? Sniff around and things like that?

SANDA. I can give it a try. The people in this neighbourhood, I understand their psychology. I know them, and they happen to show me some respect . . .

BIG MAN SHOPPER. Yes, yes, it's something I've noticed myself. For someone doing security job, you seem very well educated. One of my business partners said the same thing when she came shopping here last week.

SANDA. Thank you, sir. Well, if you're willing to have me try . . .

BIG MAN SHOPPER. We could do both. What about that? The police also have their sources you know . . .

SANDA (*shakes his head firmly*). The police know only what they want to know. They find out only what they want to find out . . . And they remember only what they find convenient to remember. We security people know them, that's why we operate separately. If you want me to handle this with our own people, we must do it our own way and that means – no police.

BIG MAN SHOPPER. All right, all right. I leave it to you. Do what you can. You will not complain of my gratitude.

SANDA. Ah yes, I was coming to that, sir. Things may move faster if we had a bit of . . . er . . . manure to spread along the ground. We'll plant the seed at once but, it would germinate much faster if . . . you understand?

BIG MAN SHOPPER. Of course, of course. (*He takes out a wallet and peels out several notes.*)

SANDA (*stopping him as he increases the amount*). No, no, this is more than enough. Good God, we're not the police. In fact . . . (*He returns a few notes.*) . . . yes, this will do very well – for preliminaries.

BIG MAN SHOPPER. No, take it. It's better you have more than enough. I don't want you being held back because of lack of . . .

SANDA. It's better this way. Just enough for expenses as we proceed. If we run against a brick wall and we have to abandon the search, then we wouldn't have wasted your money. Even my own contacts are not perfect; if I give them too much to begin with, they will think the bread is without limit. When it's over, I'll leave it entirely to you to – make them all right.

BIG MAN SHOPPER. You won't be disappointed, I promise you. Oh, let me give you my card. That way you can find me if you need further expenses . . .

SANDA. But, sir, everyone knows you here. Who doesn't know the offices of such a big man as yourself. Don't worry, sir, I know how to find you. (*Turns to the captive.*) Hey, you juvenile delinquent! Follow oga with his shopping back to his car and report here afterwards . . .

BIG MAN SHOPPER. Hen? You think that is wise? Suppose he runs away?

SANDA. Who? That one – run away? Where to? I know his mother's house – if you can call it that. More like a shack for storing firewood but – that's the way life is for many around Ita Balogun. Where is he going to run to?

> *Still dubious about the wisdom of such a decision,* BIG MAN SHOPPER *lets* BOYKO *precede him, and watches him closely all the way through the alley.*

BIG MAN SHOPPER. I'll expect to hear soon from you?

SANDA. Trust me, oga. (*He watches them go, then shouts after him.*) And don't give him any tip. Just send him back to come and face his music. We'll get the truth out of him.

TRADER (*silent chuckle*). Oga Security, shay a fit go back to my station?

SANDA. Go 'way!

> TRADER *scampers down, chuckling.* SANDA *resumes his place, and reading. A few moments pass, then* AREA TWO-FOUR *enters, carrying a small shopping bag. He takes it to* SANDA, *opens it so he can see its contents.*

TWO-FOUR. Bread no plenty; na so-so paper dey inside. Passport, passbook, files and so on and so forth. (SANDA *flicks a most cursory glance over the contents, not even taking the bag.*) Make we throway the case inside lagoon?

SANDA (*thinks for a moment*). It's good quality leather.

TWO-FOUR. Na good quality evidence – should in case the police follow the case.

SANDA. No-o. This one na *so-o-say*. No *wahala*. In any case, we musn't waste the case. We shall proceed to – find it. He's promised a large reward. Put it inside safe.

TWO-FOUR. As you like, oga.

SANDA. Right. And, from now on, see that that area around the military pay office is patrolled. Some of these car-owners think they're very smart.

> *Exit* TWO-FOUR. SANDA *picks up a journal, makes some notes inside, and ticks off a column with a flourish. He resumes his reading. Enter* MISEYI, *accompanied by her housemaid, heading for the store entrance.* SANDA *does not look up. Instead, he focuses on the high heels, then slowly raises his gaze as their owner climbs the steps, so that his eyes become level with her head as she reaches the entrance, by which time her back is turned towards him. Suddenly, he freezes. At the same moment, the woman stops, then turns round. Their eyes meet.*

SANDA (*a slow smile breaks over his face*). I was sure there was no duplicating that walk, even going up the steps, or the carriage side-view. Then of course the head profile, especially where the neck bridges it with the shoulder . . .

MISEYI. And I thought there was also no mistaking the habit of the head when hunched over a book or anything in print. But then I grew doubtful, seeing that it was hidden under a ludicrous storefront security cap – Sanda! What on earth are you doing in that outfit?

SANDA. What else? Earning a living of course.

MISEYI. This is one of your jokes? Wait a minute – no. Today is not Students' Rag Day or we'd have seen them all over the place rattling their beggars' tins for one charity or the other. So, it has to be some other kind of stunt – let's see now, what's today?

SANDA. Stunt? Students' Rag Day? What's the matter with you? Don't tell me time has stood still for you these past four years. Four? Or is it five? Yes, five years since we last spoke to each other, and you look every mature day of that passage of time.

MISEYI. You are still your unflattering old self I see, but . . .

SANDA. No. I meant that most sincerely. Time has done some lovely toning on your face, on your skin. You have bloomed beyond my wildest hopes for you – I did say, mature, didn't I? Yes, you do look mature, in the most delectable way.

MISEYI. Don't expect any grateful response from me – if what I am looking at is for real.

SANDA. This? It's real enough.

MISEYI. No, it's not.

SANDA. Yes, it is.

MISEYI. No way. It cannot be.

SANDA. Oh yes it is.

MISEYI. Sanda, ple-e-ease, explain this joke. You saw me coming, didn't you? You came shopping just like me and then you saw me from a distance. You borrowed the cap and the jacket . . .

SANDA. And the trousers? I changed from whatever I was wearing into this outfit just to tease an old friend?

Pause. They confront each other, he light-hearted, she increasingly tight-lipped as she realises that this is for real.

MISEYI. I wish I could be struck blind, suddenly, no, even before now. Or that my feet had taken me any other way but this.

SANDA (*sadly*). I can see your mind has not kept pace with the rest of you – that's a great pity.

MISEYI (*heatedly*). And your mind has stood still, Sanda! Still, still, stagnant. You are still the way you *talked*! The eternal student at heart. People grow. They develop. You . . . you . . . Christ, it makes one weep inside to look at you! Did you abandon your degree programme, one year to graduation – for this? A *megadi* uniform for what should have been . . .

SANDA. . . . an academic gown? (*Laughs.*) Now who is out of touch with change? Me or you? Do you know how many hundreds of PhDs are roaming the streets, jobless. Me, I have a full-time job. And even compared to those with jobs – my take-home pay is twice theirs any week. And when I make up my mind and decide to earn good tips, I can take home six times that pay.

MISEYI. And you're proud of that? You wear that *megadi* uniform, hold the door open for people . . .

SANDA. It's a sliding door, haven't you noticed? Automatic. It opens by itself.

MISEYI. Don't try to be funny. I'm looking at you helping big men and their women with their shopping bags, holding open their car doors while they roll in their fat bodies, and there you *are* funny, ludicrous.

SANDA. Oh no, I'm not allowed to leave my post. A simple whistle from me – (*Whistles. Three or four small boys dash in from all corners.*) – See? I try to be fair, make sure they all get a fair share of the porterage. Let's see now – you and you – (*He makes a selection.*) – Just two will do. As you see, Madame has brought her own maid, so your job is to follow her and make sure no one tries to snatch her purse. And of course you carry anything she or her maid wants you to carry, and you see her to the car – oh, I take it your car is being – er – looked after? Oh, but of course you would have come with a driv – beg pardon, ma'am – *chauffeur.* Well, there it is in action. No sweat at all. And naturally, as you're leaving, you'll sidle towards Oga Security, slip a ten or twenty-naira in his hand. And you'll be interested to know – or wouldn't you? – it isn't a naira note that some madams slip into my hand, even married ones, but a card, a slip of paper with a telephone number, and a whisper . . .

MISEYI (*turns to the maid, head flung high*). Let's go. You need a psychiatrist, Sanda. You need a good session on the couch.

SANDA. That's just what those madams whisper when they come up to me. Couldn't you have been more original?

MISEYI. Oh you're lost. You've become decadent.

SANDA. And you are – beautiful my dear. And hopelessly antiquated.

MISEYI (*stung, she spins round*). Well, instruct me then, Mr Clever! Introduce us into this . . . these – lower depths – into which you have chosen to sink. Mr Slum Artist, Street Sociologist. We shared classes, so I think we do speak the same language. I say you're nothing but a sham, a poseur, masquerading among a class to which you don't belong. You're a cheat even, you know that? Others need those tips more desperately than you, because they have no other way of earning a living. But you scrounge for the same scraps with them, don't you? So who are you to preach anything when all you do is waste the training you were given? Go on, I'm listening. You were trained at somebody's expense you know. So give us more of that old student gibberish. You think there is some nobility in this way of living, something that makes you superior to the rest of us?

They confront each other, one furious, the other smiling.

SANDA. Who said anything of nobility? Or superiority? I've merely chosen the way I want to live, what's wrong with that? I decided to return home, to where I was born. And if you knew the rest of it, oh-oh, if you only knew the rest of it, you wouldn't dream of accusing me of acting superior. (*Sighs, and turns away.*) Oh, Miseyi, go your way, as we both did five years ago. We've met by chance. I would have loved it if you had offered me a drink although, come to think of it, I should offer you hospitality, since this is my territory, my constituency. However, since things have to be this way . . . (*He doffs his cap.*) . . . enjoy your shopping, madam.

MISEYI. You failed, is that it? What you set out to do when you dropped out. You failed. You were whipped. You were to make your first million within six months – where is it?

SANDA. The waters were too murky. I couldn't swim in them.

MISEYI. Not even for the revolution? The millions were to go into the struggle, that was the whole purpose, wasn't it? Couldn't you stand a little dirt for Utopia?

SANDA (*smiling*). A little dirt. Oh, the little you know. Go, go. Go before you learn more than what your mind can take.

> MISEYI *flounces off, angry.* SANDA *returns to his bench and resumes his reading.* TRADER *watches him for some moments, fiddles around his wares in some embarrassment.*

TRADER. Hm-hm, oga, make you take time. Take time for that woman o. I no like de ting she talk at all. I no like am at all at all.

SANDA. What did she say that you don't like?

TRADER. No, not the actual ting wey she talk, na the way she talk 'am. When woman talk like that enh, make man get ready to dodge.

SANDA. We're old friends. That's the way we used to shout at each other in the university. (*Shakes his head, bewildered.*) It's amazing how we fell smoothly into the old routine, as if we parted only yesterday.

TRADER. Hn-hn. Hn-hn. As if to say I know all dat before. Still and yet, make all dat be as 'e be. Me, I just say, standby to dodge o!

> Enter a POLICEMAN, *dragging a bleeding, badly damaged man by his trouser waistband. A small crowd follows. A missile is hurled at the* VICTIM *just missing him and landing near* SANDA's *feet. One of the crowd carries a worn car tyre. The crowd is rather unusual in that each of the men has at least one hand over his crotch, while the women cover their breasts with their hands, or use one arm across both.*

SANDA. What the . . . !

> The POLICEMAN *sees possible assistance in a man in security uniform and runs towards him with his captive.*

POLICEMAN. Can you help, sir? Is there somewhere we can keep this man away from the crowd. They're determined to lynch him, although, why I should bother . . .

SANDA. What's the matter?

POLICEMAN. Missing genitals.

SANDA (*groans*). Oh, not again!

> Shouts of 'Hand him over!' 'Let's roast him here before he roasts in hell.' 'They don't deserve police protection.' 'Tyre done ready, kerosene dey plenty.'

SANDA. Stand by, Area Two-One. Send Boyko for some of ours. (*To the* POLICEMAN.) Which of them claims to be the victim?

VICTIM (*steps forward*). It's me, brother. He touched me, and it was gone.

SANDA. You are sure.

VICTIM. Am I sure? Don't I know what I left home with? And now there's absolutely nothing there. Nothing. He touched me and I felt it disappear. (*Starts crying.*)

POLICEMAN. Stop crying like a child. Stand up and behave like a man.

VICTIM. Behave like a man? Like a man? But that's the core of my problem. How do you expect me to behave like a man without it.

SANDA. And it happened after he touched you. You're sure it was this man?

VICTIM. I have witnesses. (*Approaches one of the crowd.*) That gentleman . . .

WITNESS. Hey, keep your distance.

VICTIM. What? Are you denying you . . . ?

WITNESS. I'm not denying anything. I saw it with my own eyes and I am ready to testify in court. But you don't have to touch me, do you? Just point at me from a distance.

VICTIM. Hey, what's this? (*Turns to the next person.*) What's the matter with him?

WOMAN. You heard him. Keep your distance. We all feel sorry for you, and we want to see justice done. But don't spread it around.

VICTIM. Don't spread . . . It is not an infectious disease! I've lost my manhood, that's all. What is infectious about that?

WITNESS. You never know. That's how AIDS began you know. Before you knew it, it was spreading like wildfire.

VICTIM. AIDS! The whole world has gone mad. I tell you I'm just a victim of vanishing organs. My genitals have disappeared – what has that to do with AIDS?

WOMAN (*stubbornly*). That's how AIDS began. First we didn't even have it here, in Africa. Then they said it started here. With monkeys.

WITNESS. Yeah. Green monkeys.

VICTIM. Oh my manhood! My manhood!

BARBER. It's probably making millions for his syndicate somewhere in Lagos. They work in syndicates you know. It's funny, we were just talking about it.

SANDA. Don't add fuel to this dirty fire, Mr Barber.

BARBER. You never believed me, but there it is, before your very eyes.

VICTIM. My manhood!

POLICEMAN. Look, my friend, just restore his genitals and I promise you full protection.

SANDA. Cut it out, officer! Is that the kind of example expected of you?

WITNESS. The policeman is right. We can't let even the victim loose. Suppose he touches someone else, how do we know that person's own won't also disappear?

BARBER. They're right, you know. It's a good thing you kept them both. Instead of the hard work of going round touching likely victims, you touch only one. It saves the labour. That one doesn't know he's become a carrier, so he touches another, and so on. Soon you have a hundred people running loose with no genitals, causing others to lose theirs. And meanwhile somebody sits in his mansion, spiriting millions from the Central Bank.

SANDA. You either shut up, Barber, or I terminate your occupation rights. I think you've all gone mad.

WOMAN. Have we? What of the government role in all this? Have you thought of that?

SANDA. The government. What about the government?

WOMAN. Suppose they're behind it all. It's a military government and they've been preaching population control. It's just the kind of wicked tactics they would think of.

WITNESS. They want to rule forever, don't they? What better way to do that than to emasculate all of us?

ANOTHER WITNESS. Hey! You've said something, believe me, you have said something! Since this thing started, have you seen it affect any of them? I bet they give them an injection against it before they leave their barracks. My God!

WITNESS. Don't forget the police. Look at that one. He's not afraid to touch that devil. I bet he's also innoculated. It's a plot against the civilian population.

SANDA. There's one way to stop all this nonsense. (*Approaches* VICTIM.) Watch me shake hands with him. I'll even embrace him.

VICTIM (*retreating*). Don't come near me.

SANDA. What?

VICTIM. Don't come near me. How do I know you're not one of them? After all, you're in uniform.

SANDA. Oh my God, it's an asylum!

VICTIM. I don't want you to prove anything with me.

SANDA. Well, there's nothing there, you said, so what do you stand to lose?

VICTIM. What of the other organs? I don't want them to disappear. I don't trust anyone. Just make him undo his handiwork or else leave me alone.

SANDA. All right. That's it. Take down your trousers.

VICTIM. You said what?

SANDA. I said, Take – down – your – trousers!

VICTIM. You want me to . . . before all these people?

SANDA. Why not? There is nothing there, so there is nothing to be coy about.

POLICEMAN. That's a good idea. Take them off!

WOMAN. Why didn't we think of that? Let's prove it to these unbelievers once for all. Take off your trousers and shut up their mouths.

VICTIM. You're all making fun of me. You want to expose my nakedness to all these people? (*Waves his arm around the audience.*)

WITNESS. You'll have to do it in court anyway.

VICTIM. That brother is right. This is a lunatic asylum. You actually want me to strip in public?

WITNESS. We can go inside if you like. Let's find a secluded place inside the plaza.

SANDA. Enough! That's more than enough. No one is coming in here except the policeman and the genital brothers. Everybody else, back! Go home. That's quite enough idiocy for one morning.

ACCUSED. God knows I didn't do anything.

POLICEMAN. You didn't touch him?

ACCUSED. At a crowded bus-stop? Everybody touches everybody. Everyone is squeezing everyone else to death.

SANDA (*to* TRADER). Get one of the girls. Pick one with . . . er . . . you know. I'm going to lock this one in a room with her and we'll see if the right stimulus doesn't give us results.

TRADER. I think I sabbe the very one wey fit defeat any kind *juju* attack. If she get customer. I go wait make in finish.

SANDA. And tell the boys to clear this rabble. I don't want to see any of them around when I get back. As for you, Barber, you can go with them if you want to continue spreading around that rubbish.

BARBER. Did you hear me say anything?

SANDA. You've said more than enough. It's people like you who turn the most docile crowd into mindless beasts. (*Goes in with the trio.*)

TRADER. Move, you lot. You done hear, oga. Or you want make I

set the boys on you? This no be your territory, you know.
Vamoose!

The crowd melts away, grumbling.

BARBER. The world is filled with too many unbelievers.
TRADER. Make we no quarrel o. You know say meself I believe say
something dey for dis business, but oga done say make we no
talk am again. So, no talk am again.
BARBER. All right, all right. (*Whispers to the* CYCLIST.) You see? As
if we knew this was going to happen when I began telling you
about that severed head . . .
MAMA PUT (*scoops up some steaming bean pottage with a ladle
and rounds on* BARBER, *pulling his trousers outwards by the
waistband with the other hand.*) You want me to scald your
own manhood with this hot stuff?
BARBER (*clutches his crotch*). I beg, I beg, I done shut up.

   MINSTREL *crosses the stage, singing: 'Iy a Meji Eyi J'okobo
   O'.*

   The FOREIGNER *emerges from the store, followed at a short
   distance by* SANDA. SANDA *is reading a newspaper as he walks
   back.* FOREIGNER *sees him, stops and slips a twenty-naira
   note in his hand.*

FOREIGNER. Just a small token of appreciation. Oh – and let me
leave you my card. In case you ever decide you want to change
jobs – ours is a new firm – you strike me as the kind of person we
could use.
SANDA. That is kind of you, sir.
FOREIGNER. Not at all. Be seeing you.

   *As he reaches the bottom of the steps, a rickety bus is heard
   roaring to a stop. Instantly, a huge commotion begins as a
   long-suffering crowd struggles to climb on board. The* FORE-
   IGNER *watches, reacting to the scene. Then he unslings his
   camera and begins to take pictures. The chaotic scene is*

partially reflected in the sliding doors. Shouts, curses, groans, with the CONDUCTOR'*s voice raised above the din to which he adds by banging on the side of the bus.*

SANDA (*eyes glued to the paper*). So they did it after all. They wiped Maroko settlement off the surface of the earth.

MAMA PUT. Maroko? What now? Can't they ever leave those people alone?

SANDA. They will after this. There is no more Maroko. It's in this evening paper.

TRADER. Oga, you mean they chase the people commot?

SANDA. According to this, they weren't just chased out, Trader. The entire place was flattened. Here. There are even photos. (TRADER *takes the paper.* MAMA PUT *goes across to read over his shoulder.*) Now where do a million people go to find a home?

BARBER. But they took the government to court. They won. The court ordered government to leave them alone.

MAMA PUT (*tight-lipped, walks back to her station*). It's a military government, isn't it? That means they can defy even God's commandments.

CONDUCTOR. Marine Road Apapa. Marine Road last stop. Next stop Iganmu. Four place on board. I say only four place on board . . . Iganmu next stop . . . We no fit take more than four . . . Hey! You people dey craze? I say only four place dey inside . . . Hey, mind that woman. Mind that woman! No, no load at all. We no fit take load inside. Driver, make we move. Go next stop. Move, I beg, move on! Anybody wey no commot for step, na your palava o. (*Bangs on the bus.*) Move on driver, go, go! No more space!

> *Re-enter* MISEYI. *She hesitates, then takes a decision and goes to* SANDA, *who is still distracted by the commotion from across the road.*

MISEYI. I'm sorry. That was all very childish. I think I was shocked, that's all. We didn't have to quarrel.

SANDA (*his attention is still fixed in the direction of the bus-stop*). Old habits die hard.

MISEYI. I'm getting married.

SANDA (*that does get his attention*). What?

MISEYI. Getting married. That's why I came here. To check the arrangements in the plaza.

SANDA. Oh. You mean it's you? The booking. I hadn't linked . . .

MISEYI. For tonight? Yes. Everything is tonight – the asking ceremony, the formal engagement and the traditional wedding. I didn't want an elaborate affair.

SANDA. You didn't want an elaborate . . . The street is being closed from seven. And you say that is not an elaborate affair?

MISEYI. If you knew what both parties wanted! My parents. And my fiancé himself. He has a rather ostentatious side to him. Exhibitionist even, but he manages to be sweet with it.

SANDA. Oh, it's not my business. I just never thought . . . there are three music bands in attendance, right? Good God!

MISEYI. What's the matter?

SANDA. Talking of bands suddenly reminded me – do you still play the xylophone?

MISEYI (*laughing*). Hardly ever. Not since I left college. And you? How is the bass guitar?

SANDA. Off and on, off and on. I still jam with the odd group after work.

MISEYI. You still write songs? *That* kind?

SANDA. What kind do we live? (*Waves his arms around.*) What other kind is there?

> *The brief silence is awkward for both.*

MISEYI (*wistfully*). We did have some good times.

SANDA. Life beckons, we respond. You cross another bridge tonight.

MISEYI. Yes, tonight. Everything will be over tonight, thank goodness. I put my foot down over that. Those wedding events that drag on for ever . . .

SANDA. Not even the usual follow-up church wedding?

MISEYI. Me? A white wedding? Come on, we've talked about such things often enough. You know my views.

SANDA. People change.

MISEYI. But not you. Not the immovable Sanda.

SANDA. Oh, don't be so sure. Well, who is the lucky man?

MISEYI. Why? Don't you know?

SANDA. For me, it was just another big do. I didn't bother to check. Most people just book the space anyway. My job is to look after peace and order. People make their own arrangements. So who is he?

MISEYI. You won't approve of him – he's rich. And likes to show it. But he works hard for his money. Here. (*Thrusts an envelope at him.*) That's your invitation, if you feel like coming to lend moral support. I mean it, you'll be more than welcome – for old times' sake.

SANDA. Thanks. But I'll be here anyway. I'm on duty. I work overtime any time there's a function in the plaza. I enjoy them. The tips are overwhelming.

> *Increased commotion as the bus takes off.* SANDA *is just easing the card out of the envelope when a* PASSENGER's *scream rips through the scene. Dropping the card,* SANDA *races out in the direction of the scream.*

PASSENGER'S VOICE. Dey done kill me. Dey done kill me. Dey done take the only thing I get for this world. Wicked people, dey done take my life. I get nothing left, nothing in the world. No, lef' me, lef' me make I die. Dey done kill me, dey done finish my life. (*Violent scream.*) No touch am! Take your hand commot, I say make nobody touch am! I go curse anybody wey touch am. In hand go wither for in body, in hand no go do better thing for the world. I say make you commot your hand . . . !

> *The sound ceases abruptly.* MISEYI *descends a step or two, so that she is standing by the* FOREIGNER *as, a few moments later,* SANDA *re-enters, carrying the limp body of a* PASSENGER *in his*

arms. He climbs the steps and enters the store, TRADER *following with a small bundle wrapped in a shawl.* MAMA PUT *moves rapidly towards him.*

MISEYI. Sanda! (*He does not respond.*)

FOREIGNER. What happened?

TRADER (*lifts the bundle towards him, without stopping*). This used to be dat woman pikin. They done trample am to death.

MAMA PUT *makes to take the bundle from him but* MISEYI *gets to it first. They follow* SANDA *into the store.*

MISEYI (*to Maid*). No, you get the driver. Meet me at the back of the plaza.

TRADER *sits on the step, holding his head. Enter* MINSTREL.

MINSTREL. Wey Oga Security? I hear all dat noise. Wetin happen?

TRADER. Oga dey inside.

MINSTREL. Me, I tire small. (*Sits on the step and unslings his kanango.*)

TRADER. Now wetin dat woman go tell in husband when she reach home?

MINSTREL (*disturbed. Appears to be listening hard*). What's the matter? Everything seems suddenly quiet. Did something bad happen? What was the woman screaming about? I was too far off to make it all out but . . . there was so much pain in the air.

BARBER. Nothing much happened, my friend, nothing unusual. Go on, sing that old favourite you sang for us the day Mama Put's daughter took her communion. Do you remember the party we had here? Three full pots of beans and plantain Mama Put cooked for the neighbourhood, with solid chunks of fried pork. And was she raging when Sanda tried to pay for everything?

TRADER (*cheering up a little*). Yeah. Dat Mama Put, she sure get temper.

MINSTREL *begins to sing: 'Omo L'aso'. Towards the end of the song,* SANDA *returns and resumes his seat on the stool.* MAMA

PUT *follows moments after. He picks up a magazine and tries to concentrate on it. Puts it down after some moments. Enter the* GIRL, *back from school.*

MAMA PUT. You're back early. Weren't you given any after-school assignment?

GIRL. But Mama, you said I was to return right away.

MAMA PUT (*for a moment, she is puzzled*). Oh yes. That dream of mine, I suppose. Dreams make me nervous, that's true. But the grief belonged to someone else. I was smothered by its approach, but the grief was elsewhere. Are you hungry?

The GIRL *nods. She serves her food from the pot.* SANDA *watches both.*

It's a hard school we attend here, girl, so be sure to enjoy yours. Work hard at your books, but also enjoy what fun is still left in your schools. Here, don't use your hand. Use the fork and knife like you do at school. Oh, I know. I snatch the knife from you sometimes and prefer to eat from a clay bowl, but that is only when I remember . . . I even prefer clay pots for cooking. But it's not that I refuse to touch metal. After all, I prepare the meat with this heirloom. I use it to cut up vegetables. (*She grips the bayonet hard.*) And I keep it handy. It's a hard school we go to, a hard school in a heartless city, and today one child didn't even get to enjoy her childhood.

SANDA. Where is Boyko?

BOYKO. I dey here, oga.

SANDA (*after what appears to be a thoughtful inspection*). Hm. Look at him after a mere three years. When he came, he was no bigger than the bundle Miseyi has just managed to restore to that despairing woman. But he was actually seven years old, only, there was nothing on him you could call flesh. Wasn't it you who first spotted him, Trader, rooting in this very gutter for something to eat. You remember what he looked like?

TRADER. Na Barber first see am. But like you said, oga, in bone no get flesh.

SANDA. I vomited, just to watch him pick that thing out of that gutter. I had no idea he would actually put it in his mouth. But he did. Wiped it against his thigh, then stuck it in his mouth, and chewed away. By the time Barber screamed out loud it was too late to stop him. I threw up.

BARBER. You did, I remember.

SANDA. You do, do you? You see, I wonder sometimes, maybe I should have turned my back on that sight. We save some, yes, but others kill them anyway. They kill them before, or they kill them afterwards. It doesn't seem to make much difference, because we all join hands to kill them anyway. In other places, they do it differently of course. Bogota. Or Rio de Janeiro, where our businessmen make an annual date with the carnival, Boyko would be dead in one of those places. They have death squads over there for people like him. For picking up food from the gutter, he'd be marked down for death. Class sanitation, right from infancy. (*He looks increasingly troubled.*) Mama Put is right. We live in a cruel land. A cruel time in a cruel land. To breathe at all is to breed cruelty, to scatter the spores of hardcore, unsullied cruelty. Hardcore as in pornography. Innocence means death.

BOYKO. You get assignment for me, oga?

SANDA. What? Oh no, sorry. Oh yes, I want you to give more time to that flute. If you practise less than four hours a day, I'll crack your head. Now go and give Ma Put a hand. Everyone must pack up earlier than usual. (BOYKO *crosses over to* MAMA PUT's *stall.*) The police and soldiers will be here soon to seal up the streets. And the prison detail to clean up. The affluent are about to take over the neighbourhood, then they'll restore it to us again.

> Enter JUDGE, *but startlingly transformed. His long hair has been permed and curled so it actually looks like a judicial wig. He also has on the semblance of a purple robe, certainly much the worse for wear. The* BARBER *looks the most shocked and displeased, and is first to recover his voice.*

BARBER. Mama Put . . . Oga Security . . . do you people see what I'm looking at? Do you see how Judge has slighted me?

TRADER. You? Wetin be your own for this *alawada* man?

BARBER. Haven't you got eyes in your head? Where did he get that hair treatment? Where? Did you see him get up from my chair? Has he not bypassed my own salon and taken his custom to some total stranger? Security, is this how we are supposed to help one another here? Where did you go anyway? Look at what they did to your head? And you sat down and let some amateur . . .

JUDGE. Where are your curlers?

BARBER. What?

JUDGE. Curlers. Rollers. Hot comb. Relaxers etcetera. The trouble with the world is that everyone refuses to accept their limitations. You think a high court judge goes to some wayside barber's shack to perfect the presence that may pass sentence of life and death? In derelict spaces and makeshift hovels?

BARBER. My salon! Do you all hear him? He's calling my salon a hovel.

JUDGE. Don't be so parochial, man! The majesty of the law discriminates, but is impartial. It recognises neither friend nor foe, stranger or relations. Majesty! Ma – jes – ty. (*Beatific smile.*) Can you conceive it? The ma-jes-ty of the law. I told Trader I was set on the journey to souls' kingdom – he should have passed the word round, then you would have been forewarned. Still, I shall not distance myself altogether, have no fears on that score. And I shall prove it to you. You see – (*Wagging his finger.*) – I thought of you all the time. Sitting under the dryer, my scalp massaged by trained fingers, I thought of you.

> Goes to the BARBER's chair and faces the CYCLIST. He scampers up and JUDGE takes his place. CYCLIST moves into MAMA PUT's corner. From the recesses of his robe, JUDGE produces a small plastic pouch.

Here. Sprinkle this on. I saved the final treatment for you.

BARBER (*suspiciously*). What is it?

JUDGE. You can see there is something missing up there, can't you? (*Pointing at his head.*)

BARBER. Oh yeah, we all know that.

JUDGE. Naturally, a professional like you would spot it right away. Yes, the judicial wig must undergo some ageing process. Use that!

> BARBER *unties the pouch, sniffs, then takes some of the powdery content between his fingers.*

BARBER. This feels like ashes.

JUDGE. The finest and the best. (*Points.*) Scooped it up from Mama Put's ash mound before I set off. Spent all morning sifting out the cinders and grosser particles. What you have there is fire in absolute purity, purged of passion, divorced of its past. It is the pure element that is fire, but without the heat, its destructive career subsumed in serenity. Sprinkle it on. Spread it evenly from strand to strand.

BARBER. Look, I'll use the aftershave talcum powder. It's free of charge, in case it's the money you are worried about. (*About to throw it away.*)

JUDGE. Don't! Don't you dare!

BARBER. How can I use this stuff? It's against all my professional instinct. I am still hurt, I can't deny that. But, anyway you look at it, this is a work of art. Maybe I would need time to master the technique to produce something like this but, no, I can't do it. It's desecration.

JUDGE. You're a fool. No, you're blind. Blinder than that singing beggar over there. Give it back. (*Snatches it from him.*) Security.

SANDA. Yes, Judge.

JUDGE. May I ask the favour of the loan of your young jack-of-all-trades for a short spell.

SANDA. Boyko, attend to the Judge. But you can't keep him too long. He's helping with the packing up.

JUDGE. I thank you. Here, boy.

BARBER. Not in my chair!

TRADER. Come on, make you humour the man now.

BARBER. I have my professional pride. I can't allow him to desecrate my salon.

MAMA PUT. You know he won't give us any peace of mind; let him have his fun. If a customer comes, I promise I'll make him give way.

SANDA. Do us all a favour, Barber.

BARBER (*grudgingly*). All right, all right. Let's get it done with and get him off my chair.

JUDGE. You will be proud to remember this moment, my friend. You have all, in many ways, contributed to this last act of my transfiguration. Here, boy. Sprinkle it gently, then use this comb to distribute the fire dust evenly along the strands of majesty. (*Produces a tiny comb from his pocket and hands it over. Leans his head back on the head rest, closes his eyes and sighs with content.*)

TRADER. The only thing wey I no understand be, how 'e get money for pay dat kind hairdresser. Only proper saloon fit do that kind hairstyle.

SANDA. Does anything about the Judge still surprise you?

TRADER. Oga, you think say he be actually judge before. He siddon court dey pass judgement?

SANDA. No-o. I thought you all knew all about him.

TRADER. No. Na so 'e dey here like everybody else. Just as you come meet all of we. Nobody dey ask questions but, this time, I jus' wan' know.

SANDA. He was never a judge. But he was a lawyer. And he got debarred.

TRADER. De-wetin?

SANDA. Debarred. Struck off the roll of lawyers. Not allowed to practise.

TRADER. Ah! Wetin 'e do?

SANDA. I've forgotten. It was a long time ago. I was just a schoolboy at the time.

TRADER (*chuckling*). You self, oga? Is so difficult to see you inside school uniform, dey carry books go school, den come home do homework like Mama Put in daughter.

SANDA. Why? Why is that so difficult to believe?

TRADER. E be like say na for dat stool you dey since de day den born you, just siddon dere dey read book and magazine. And even yet, all the time person tink you dey read, your eyes dey look everything going on around here.

SANDA (*thoughtfully*). Me too. There are days when I feel I have never been anywhere else but here. But then, I was born and raised here. I only turned expatriate through boarding-school, then college . . .

TRADER. The neighbourhood owe you plenty. Until you come here begin organise everybody, we just dey run about like chicken wey no get head.

SANDA (*his eyes on* BOYKO). I wonder sometimes, Trader. I wonder sometimes if I'm in the right place or doing the right thing.

> TRADER *looks worried, gives him a searching look. Turns away slowly and begins to fiddle with his wares.*
>
> *Approaching, the prison detail. The* WARDER's *voice is heard keeping the group in order: 'Left – Right – Left – Right – Left – Right – Single File – Left – No lagging. No hanging back! You there – Left – Right . . . ' Soon, they are reflected in the doors.*

SANDA. Here they come. Better get the welfare package ready for them to take back.

TRADER. Anytin special you want make I put?

SANDA. Just make sure there's plenty of their local currency.

TRADER (*chuckles*). Independent Republic of Kirikiri Maximum: hard currency, Sirocco High Filter; local, Elephant tusk. Black market – raw tobacco leaf.

WARDER'S VOICE. Left – Right – Left – Right –

PRISONERS (*singsong*).

> Lefu – Rete – Lefu. Lefu – Rete – Lefu.
> Ati warder, at'elewon

Ikan na ni wa
Ati soja, at'olopa
Ole paraku
Eni a ri mu la l'edi mo
Ole mbe l'ode
Jaguda nwo khaki
Olosa General
Major adana
A gba'ni lo ju gba'ya al'aya
A lo ni l'owo, gba'le on'ile
Riba l'otun, egunje l'osi
Aiye yin mbe ni bi o
Aiye yin mbe l'ewon
Lefu – Rete – Lefu. Lefu – Rete – Lefu.

WARDER. Left – Right – Left – Right – Mind your tongues. You're in public. Careless talk or careless singing, it's a crime of treason. Sorry, sedition – well, one of them anyway, the SSS will find something to hang on you. Left – Right – Don't look for trouble. Left – Right – Don't get me in trouble. Left – Right. I don't want companionship in misery – certainly not yours! And don't forget your remission. Don't sing yourselves out of possible remission. This is a no-nonsense government, don't fool around with military feeling – if they have any.

PRISONERS:

Lefu – Rete – Lefu. Lefu – Rete – Lefu
Eru o b'odo. Lefu – Rete. Mo ti w'ewon
Lefu – Rete. Moti g'oke, mo ti so
Faka-fiki faka fi
Aginju o joju, papa o ya'nu
Se b'afoda nti gada?
Afoda l'ejo elewon
Mo ti w'ole na, mo ti gba number
Sapagiri nbe n'ikun
A t'odo Oya, a t'ibu osa
Afoda nt'afefe lele

Railway nsere ni, ko s'ohun t'oju o riri
Wole-wole nparo ni
Atan l'atan nje.
Tanwiji mbe n'isale amu
O ba a se ju t'esi
Lefu – Rete – Lefu. Lefu – Rete – Lefu.
Soja oselu, jaguda paali
Baba bilisi. Oo gbe'bon mo
Oo ja'gun la, kontirakiti lo nle kiri.

WARDER. Stand at ease! Stand easy! Trouble makers I don't want. Trouble makers I don't like. Watch your tongues. Even the potholes have ears. Don't provoke the khaki boys. Warm up and get going. Songido, get them started!

PRISONERS (*gyrating into a single file, rap-style chant*).
So we'll do the army conga
To make the work go faster
Prison is the land of free speech
Dungeon inmates are out of reach
Except for experts sworn to teach
And do-good preachers come to preach
Co-co-co-conga Co-co-co-conga

So knack us the rulers' conga rap
Give us the good old military crap
Don't look too far for the credibility gap
It's the hole beneath the General's cap.
Songido, lead off man, we're waiting
Sing us that one with an X-rating.
Co-co-co-conga Co-co-co-conga.

PRISONER 1 (*looks in the direction of* SANDA). Make I ask permission from Oga Security first. Na in get de copyright after all. (SANDA *waves them to go ahead.*) OK, OK, make you give man some solid funky conga beat.

They set up a beat with cutlasses, iron files and dustbin covers.

My friends, come gather round
And dig the latest sound
It's a universal drumbeat
In tune with every heartbeat
   My friends, come gather round
   And dig the latest sound

Invented by a soldier
In a land where flows the Niger
It's the ideology conga
That makes a nation stronger
   Invented by a soldier
   In a land that flows the Niger.

A little to the Left – shake!
A little to the Right – shake!
Red Flag or Imperial Purple
All you need is a waist that's supple
   A little to the Left – shake!
   A little to the Right – shake!

Learn from the Soviet Union
Don't stick to doomed opinion
You must swim with the tide
And take your people for the ride
   A little to the Left – Right
   A little to the Right – Left

The conga law of equity
Yields economic parity
You squeeze the left and waste
Its resources on the right caste
   A little to the Left *etc*.

It's revolutionary
For minds that are visionary
Who needs the aid of opium

Until the next millenium?
  A little to the Left *etc.*

The conga shuns restraint
No room for the plaster saint
Be you National Exchequer,
Or a budding nation wrecker
  A little to the Left *etc.*

The Naira's doing Right
It's floating out of sight
There's virtue in thrift
No purchasing power Left
  A little to the Left – Right.

Drugs have fled the clinic
Hospitals ain't no picnic
But fortunes are made
In the mortuary trade
  A little to the Left *etc.*

The boat has left its course – No!
The boat is right on course – No!
It's turning round in a circle
Like a demonstration vehicle
  A little to the Left *etc.*

The ship of state is healing
Dismiss that sinking feeling
How dare you say disaster?
It's a national fiesta!
  A little to the Left *etc.*

It's truly orgiastic
A pendulum to mimic
The ruling minds are static
But the balls are swinging frantic
  A little to the Left *etc.*

Drifting, drifting, drifting.
How sweet is simply drifting
I'll see you around
When the ship goes down
    Drifting, drifting, drifting.

How sweet is simply drifting
Drifting, drifting, drifting . . .

PRISONER 2. At least, prison get stability. I sorry too much for all these people wey still dey outside. How den dey manage survive, enh? How anybody dey manage?

WARDER. You've had your fun, right? I heard nothing. I was taking a pee while you were warming up to begin work. The regulations permit a five-minute warming-up session and a five-minute cool-down session per hour. You've used up both. Now get to work. Clean up this pigsty! And don't forget I've got my eyes peeled for any malingerers. Trusty!

PRISONER 1. Oga warder.

WARDER. Take over. (*Goes off some distance and sits down, lights a cigarette.*)

PRISONER 1. Twenty minutes per each, that na the deal wey I make with warder. I take the first shift. All of una, begin work. Clean up the rubbish.

They go off in different directions, picking up debris in the most desultory fashion. PRISONER 1 *moves towards* SANDA, *a broad, expectant beam on his face.*

Oga mi!

SANDA *nods towards* TRADER. PRISONER 1 *moves towards him.*

PRISONER 1. Shey we do justice small to that your conga?

SANDA. Not bad. Not bad.

PRISONER 1. You get new one for us?

SANDA. It's in the welfare package. You'll find the cassette inside the loaf of bread.

PRISONER 1. Trust oga! But make you no forget your promise o. When we commot, you must put us for inside that band you wan' form. We be four wey done begin learn instruments. My own na guitar. Jacko done begin expert for the saxophone wey you buy am.

SANDA. We'll see, we'll see.

PRISONER 1. Mama Put, I dey come o. Make you put me two naira *konkere* at the ready. Two meat. (*Shaking his head.*) When man taste Mama Put *konkere*, e no go believe say na de same bean den dey take make we own *sapagiri* for prison. And one shot of Number One, plus one bottle for takeaway. No worry for hurry, oga warder done give us twenty minute each. Na me take first turn. (*Sees the* JUDGE *for the first time, his mouth open in surprise.*) Ah-ah. But no to we own very judge na in dis?

TRADER. Na im. (*Hands him the packet.*)

PRISONER 1. Why e go do in hair like that come dey frighten person? Abi 'in craze done reach top of television aerial *pata-pata*?

> TRADER *shrugs.* PRISONER 1 *eyes* JUDGE *warily as he moves to* MAMA PUT'*s corner.*

Mr Judge, how now? Why you come dey do dis kin' show? E fit frighten person make 'e begin think dey done carry am go back inside court.

> *Reaches out for the bowl of food in* MAMA PUT'*s hand but she stretches out her other hand without a word.*

Ah, sorry Mama, I forget say na cash before carry.

> *Loosens the rope of his shorts, manipulates an inner lining and fishes out some money.*

Na seven of us dey come, so make you count am correct o.

> *He begins eating, rapidly, casting dubious glances at* JUDGE.

But Judge, you still dey do your circuit – er – wetin you dey call am now – clinics? Yes, circuit clinics. The one for remand prisoners.

JUDGE. Why not? Any time I encounter the rodents in open air, like today, I let them nibble at the loaf of liberation. I heard your group would be marched here to clean up the neighbourhood. Are you interested in instructions?

PRISONER 1. Me? No. I done receive my sentence long time ago. Only eleven more months to go.

JUDGE. Independence Day is just round the corner. Does that mean nothing to you?

PRISONER 1. Sure. Na dat day dem go put less water and one extra meat for stew and sometime even less stone for inside the *sapagiri*. And of course all the imams and Christian preacher go come nuisance themselves with reformation and redemption and patriotic talk-talk.

JUDGE. Amnesty. Doesn't the gracious wand of amnesty touch some of you on the national occasion?

PRISONER (*hisses*). Oh, that one. Anyone wey want commot prison for that amnesty door go take short cut to lunatic asylum. Wise person no dey hope inside prison. (*Points to the number on his chest.*) That code na my release date. Anything else, I no dey think am.

JUDGE. You're a fool. The prerogative of mercy is always open, and open to all. You only have to ensure that you are noticed, that's all. You must be noticed. You have to undergo a change. Visible change. And there are even more chances under a military regime. A governor's birthday. A hundred days in office. A year's successful tenure. His wife producing a male son – preferably twins. Anniversary of Coup. Christmas, Id-el-Fitr. Rhamaddan. New Year's Day. Army Day. Navy Day. Remembrance Day – you see, the Military have far more to celebrate than your ordinary civilian mortal.

PRISONER 1. En-hen. Thas more like our Judge. When I see you for that dress and wig, I fear you done become real judge, those wicked people wey no dey hear Sorry, I no go do so again, sir. Now you done begin talk like your real person.

JUDGE. What religion are you?

PRISONER 1. Na Christian. At least na inside Christian family den born me.

JUDGE. How often does the prison chaplain visit?

PRISONER 1. It depends. Every Sunday for sure, but e dey come take bible and catechism classes, sometimes three times a week. He can come every day if people get interest.

JUDGE. Then waste no more time. Persuade him that you have begun the journey to souls' kingdom. You're in luck. In me you have found the ideal travelling companion.

PRISONER 1. Wetin dat?

JUDGE. We shall make the journey together. Yours, of course, will be fake, but then your life is already a fake, isn't it? Faking new demons just to get out of prison should be no problem for you. Revelation, that's the key. Let your chaplain believe that you have a revelation.

PRISONER 1 (sighs). My time is almost up, Judge.

JUDGE. Eleven months to go, you said.

PRISONER 1. No, I mean this time I get siddon chop for Mama Put. Now now. For this very today. The twenty minute warder allow person make we disappear, go where we want. We fit spend that time with wife or girlfriend, you know. Is all matter of luck. Or arrangement. You get the money, you get assignment to where you want. Sometime those officers, dem dey auction the assignment, give am to highest bidder. De moment I hear say work dey for Broad Street, me I done begin negotiate for am, because I know Oga Sanda go do us well. Now I done chop belleful. Master Sanda's takeaway dey for my hand, and is nearly time to join my mates. All dis one you dey talk. I no get time for am.

JUDGE. You do not wish to take advantage of the Prerogative? Do you realise that it is even higher than the MA-JE-STY of the law. Even I do not yet aspire to such a plane, but I have begun the journey, right from this morning. I offer you the honour of serving as my guinea pig.

PRISONER I (*rising*). Hey, hey, watch your mouth. Na me you dey call pig? You people, make you warn this your Judge enh . . .

JUDGE. Go away. A mere shell of being, nothing more. A no-man's wilderness inhabited by phantoms. Your fate is to become a born-again, the genuine thing. A hideous bore. Revelation will come to you on a forlorn road, and you will clutch it to your bosom, cradling and naming it – so predictably – a jewel of inestimable value. It will come like a Mercedes Benz with blazing headlamps on a pitch dark night. The door will open and a mysterious stranger will invite you in, and you will enter, blind as a bat from the penetration of the lamps. But you will never be in the driver's seat.

> *Enter another* PRISONER, *sees the first and jerks his head towards exit.* PRISONER I *starts to leave, still scowling at the* JUDGE. *He plucks a packet of cigarettes from his parcel and hands it over.*

PRISONER I. Na you and Jacko go share that one. No forget to thank Master Sanda. I done pay Mama Put for all of una. As for that crazeman, if 'e yap you like e just yap me, make you no waste time for reply am. Just dust am one for me because he owe me one. Me, guinea pig. Nonsense!

> *A ragged procession is reflected on the doors. Men, women and children, carrying baskets, boxes, rolled-up beddings, bed springs, cupboards, chairs, clutching all kinds of personal possessions. Interspersed among them are the occasional lorries, equally laden to the top, with people perched precariously on top and among the loads. Wheelbarrows, omolanke, a tractor with trailer, also loaded with human and domestic cargo, the odd television set and antenna protruding from among baskets and sacks – An animated 'battered humanity' mural of a disorderly evacuation, maybe after an earthquake, from which an assortment of possessions have been salvaged.*

JUDGE (*raises his head slowly to stare, like others*). And what is that desolate throng? (*The procession continues, seemingly endless. He seizes a pair of clippers and bangs it thrice on the table, formally.*) Cou-ou-ou-ou-ou-ourt! The witness will answer all questions put to him and address the bench only. I said, what is that dismal throng?

BARBER. Hey, that's my work tool. (*Snatches it off him.*) If you damage it, don't imagine I shan't make you pay for it.

JUDGE. I'll deal later with this act of contempt. Meantime, I want some answers. (*Leaps up and disappears through the auditorium.*)

MAMA PUT. I hoped I had escaped such sights for ever. While the Civil War lasted, oh yes. It was like that for us most of the time. First the Biafrans who insisted we were part of them. We packed our belongings and drifted to the villages. Then the Federal Army came with their gospel of liberation. So we trooped back, just like that. Then the Biafran army returned and back we went on the roads, along bush paths, knee-deep in swamps and foraging for food like beasts of the forests. And yet again, the Federals counter-attacked, and we were told that this time, the enemy was gone for good. Not that the killings ever stopped. Both sides seemed to enjoy playing at judge and executioner. Private scores were settled as former friends and even relations denounced one another.

SANDA. I wish I could answer his question.

TRADER. Which question, oga?

SANDA. The Judge. He asked, who are this throng? This humanity?

TRADER (*puzzled*). But you know who they be, oga, na dem be the people of Maroko wey government force commot this morning.

SANDA. That's a million people, Trader. A million people within a certain environ called Lagos. Do you know them?

TRADER. How can? I no dey live inside Maroko. But we know some of them, oga, you know some of them dey come join us sometimes when we get – er – action and we want reinforcement.

SANDA. That doesn't answer the Judge's question – who are they? That's a million people you know. Look at this small group passing through Broad Street, *who* are they? And the others, drifting all over the face of Lagos. A million, that's mere statistics, but a million *people* – yes, the Judge was right. *Who* are they?

TRADER. Oga, I no sabbe this kind question you dey ask at all.

MAMA PUT (*her eyes on the passing throng*). Don't ever forget this knife, girl, don't ever forsake its history. They teach you history in school but this school is different, and the history I teach you is yours, just yours. It belongs to one one else. Look at it. They call it a bayonet. You've got that? Bay-on-et. You'd think I would hate it, keep away from all things of steel, especially this. But I kept it. You can see I use it to cut the vegetables and the meat. But it was this knife that killed my brother, so I keep it to remind me, yes, just to remind me. Because he died trying to stop them from raping me. The liberators, you know. The ones who came to liberate us. They flung him against the wall, then one of them plunged this knife in his heart. It was a quick death. There was not much to be thankful for during that war, but that was one. A quick death. They left the knife in his body and drove away in his car.

SANDA. The war is over now, Ma Put, the war is over.

MAMA PUT. Is it? Then tell me what is that procession passing through? What force was it that expelled them? Is this a sight one encounters in peace time?

SANDA. Some countries have it every year – Ethiopia for one. Such sights are common enough where droughts ravage the land and governments do not care. The whole world predicts the drought but, it's always news to those in charge.

MAMA PUT. Even that is war, then. It's war of a different kind. It is war of a kind governments declare against their people for no reason. We're too soft. We have to learn to be part of this thing here. If I had my way I'd make my girl take one to school in her schoolbag. We all need something like this lodged in our innocence.

A MILITARY OFFICER *enters from the direction in which the* JUDGE *made his exit, takes the steps two at a time, furiously. At the top he pauses, looks in the direction from which he has just emerged, scowling in rage, straightens out his uniform which is slightly askew, flicks off invisible dust from his sleeves, vigorously rubs off some invisible stain from his shoulder. His* AIDE-DE-CAMP *comes panting up after him from the same direction, and he spins round to face him.*

MILITARY OFFICER. Don't tell me you've done with him already.

ADC. The others are taking care of him, sir.

MILITARY OFFICER. I said you were to take personal charge.

ADC. I did, sir. And I left them very specific instructions, sir. I made sure he was bundled into the car boot before I left. (*Displays car keys.*) I secured the boot myself.

MILITARY OFFICER. You locked him in the boot, then what?

ADC. I thought we'd take him to the nearest police station, sir.

MILITARY OFFICER. On what charge?

ADC. Interference I thought you said, sir. Interfering with your er . . . your control of the evacuees.

MILITARY OFFICER (*between his teeth*). I ought to have you court-martialled. I ordered you to stay and handle it personally. Personally! And you want to take him to a police station where he'll intimidate them and regain his freedom? The fool interfered with my uniform. He touched it – do you understand that? He pulled my sleeve, he placed his bloody civilian hands on my uniform. And all you want to do is take him to the police station? Didn't you hear me say he was to be given the special treatment?

ADC (*salutes*). I'm sorry, sir, I didn't catch that part, there was so much commotion all around. I shall attend to it at once. (*Turns smartly to go.*)

MILITARY OFFICER. Wait. You say you have him in the boot already?

ADC. Securely locked, sir.

MILITARY OFFICER. It won't do to bring him out now and begin giving him a thrashing. There's bound to be one of these busybody upstarts calling themselves journalists who'll start publishing lies about what never happened. (*Points to the cannister hooked onto the soldier's belt.*) Mace him! Open the car boot, spray his face thoroughly and close it back. We'll take him to the barracks afterwards and then he'll begin his course of instructions. Get moving.

SANDA. Is there some trouble, officer? Can I be of help?

MILITARY OFFICER. Just some stupid judge who left his court to come and interfere with my operations.

SANDA. A judge?

MILITARY OFFICER. This section of Broad Street is to be blocked in an hour. I come here to supervise the arrangments and what do I meet? A bunch of Maroko refugees and their filthy loads clogging up the place. So I order them to move on. They are stretched out all the way to the Marina – they must have come up the Marina through Victoria Island – it would take at least an hour at the slow pace they're moving, and some of them are already thinking of camping under the flyway. Under the flyway! The party here is supposed to spill over to the flyover and down to Ita Balogun . . .

SANDA. Yes, yes, officer, this judge . . .

MILITARY OFFICER. He leaves his court and tries to interfere. Maybe he thought I would be impressed by his wig and robes – dirty robes I must say. Says a lot about the quality of judges we have on the bench these days. Probably slipped into the nearest bar for a quick one and couldn't find his way back. Do you know, he didn't even have any shoes on. He was in such a hurry to challenge my authority, he must have left them in the bar.

SANDA (*throws a brief but urgent nod at* TRADER, *who disappears*). Officer, there are no courts in this area.

MILITARY OFFICER. Typical of their judicial hypocrisy. Goes where
he's not known to get thoroughly soused. Maybe that's where he
holds his clandestine courts – you know, where the real judge-
ments are dispensed. They're all so corrupt they even hold parallel
courts. You know, where the only legal argument is naira.

SANDA (*laughing*). That bad?

MILITARY OFFICER. You had better believe it!

SANDA. But surely, officer, not in judicial robes.

MILITARY OFFICER. He was in his robes and a wig, I tell you . . .

SANDA. Are you sure he was not a vagrant? One of those . . . er . . .
touched in the head? Maybe even one of the people displaced
from Maroko.

MILITARY OFFICER. That would only make the matter worse for
him. (*Almost screaming.*) He TOUCHED my uniform. Can you
imagine one of those Maroko vermin desecrating my uniform.
For his own sake, I hope he is a genuine judge.

SANDA (*smiling*). Well, I hope so too, officer. Imagine, that would
really be an *infradig*. A common tramp. Maybe even a lunatic
escaped from some institution . . .

MILITARY OFFICER (*taken with sudden recollection*). Wait . . . a
. . . minute. He . . . now that I think of it . . . his manner . . . I
mean, what was that gibberish running from his mouth? Something about prerogative of mercy but, no, not in any way that
made sense. Good God! You mean he could have been one of
those street lunatics? He wasn't wearing any shoes and his – er –
robes, yes that did look rather tatty. But the wig was clean, well
groomed. Still . . . he kept tugging at my sleeve. He kept pawing
my uniform!

SANDA. I would put it all out of my mind, officer. Madmen or
vagrants or Maroko squatters – all they need is a dose of strong
action. So you finally sorted out Maroko?

MILITARY OFFICER (*instantly recovered*). Oh they surely got what
was coming to them. They had to go. I mean, even in their own
interest. That place was unhealthy for human habitation. The
government promised to relocate them but no, their leaders went

to see the new locations only to return and incite their people to reject them. Said they were too swampy, too isolated, no infrastructures, too this and not enough that. What did they expect? Four-star hotels? That's when we ordered the police to stand aside and leave the job to professionals. That place should have been sanitized ages ago, but the bloody civilian government kept pussyfooting and allowing technical and pseudo-legal delays to obstruct development plans. That's where a military government is really godsent, whatever anyone says.

SANDA. So Maroko is really gone? Gone for good?

MILITARY OFFICER. Didn't you see the bonfire? We didn't merely bulldoze it, we dynamited every stubborn wall, then set fire to the rubble. That place was disease ridden! No point developing it for decent citizens only to have them die of some lingering viruses from way back. Those squatters might be immune to anything but we have to think of the future residents. We took them by surprise. They woke up as usual but found themselves staring into the muzzles of guns. Few of them had any time to pick up their belongings.

SANDA. They had no warning at all?

MILITARY OFFICER. They've had masses of warning under the civilian regime, even some feeble, half-hearted eviction attempts. But the law courts always interfered. So, as the good book says, the fire next time! If you'd got up early enough you'd have seen the flames against the skyline. Gave Lagosians quite a spectacular sunrise. Lit it up for miles around as if an atom bomb had been exploded on the beach. I tell you, it was worth several weeks of training for our boys – you never know when such experience will come in useful. (*Strains to make out signs of his* ADC.) Now where's my fellow? Doesn't take that long to mace one hoodlum.

SANDA. It's quite crowded out there. He may have problems getting through. But, officer, I hope you don't mind my curiosity . . .

MILITARY OFFICER. Not at all, not at all. What do you want to know?

SANDA. What is Maroko being turned into? The rumour we heard was that the island was sitting on oil.

MILITARY OFFICER. Oh, we know of those rumours. No. Not a drop of the black gold in that area. But it's prime residential area, right on the lagoon. Oh yes, and that was something else – the sea could have risen any time and overwhelmed those stupid residents in their tin and wooden shacks. Think of the scale of the disaster! I mean, they're human beings after all. And some families have lived there over three generations. They deserve something better than a watery grave.

SANDA. You see. The media never mentioned that.

MILITARY OFFICER. The media is prejudiced. Simply prejudiced and irresponsible. But we'll deal with them in our own good time. We've worked out plans to deal with their excesses just as we've perfected plans for holding back the sea from Maroko. End the hundred or so years of neglect and decay, transform it from a breeding ground for armed robbers, drug dealers and all kinds of undesirables. You know, we couldn't even be sure that the people living there are Nigerians. Many of them could jolly well be aliens! Well, that's the end of that national embarrassment. You won't recognise it when we've completed the transformation.

SANDA. I'm sure of it.

MILITARY OFFICER. Now where in hell are . . . or – should I say – what the hell!

> *The ADC has entered, accompanied by another soldier. They look very much the worse for wear. They race up the stairs and salute.*

ADC. Permission to make report, sir.

MILITARY OFFICER. I'm waiting.

ADC. I have to report that the prisoner has escaped.

MILITARY OFFICER. Escaped? Didn't I order you to mace him unconscious?

ADC. He was unconscious, sir.

MILITARY OFFICER. Then how did he escape?

ADC. Sorry, sir, I think I put it rather badly. He didn't actually escape, sir, he was rescued.

MILITARY OFFICER. Rescued. (*Mirthless laughter*.) And by whom, may I ask? His pot-bellied colleagues on the bench? Or the Nigerian Bar Association? Yes, just who effected this rescue against a fifty-strong detachment from the crack regiment of the Nigerian army. Rescued in the presence of a fifty-strong military presence? That's nearly company strength, officer.

ADC. It was the Area Boys sir. We were overwhelmed before I could call for reinforcements – you will recall, sir, that we had positioned our men in all the strategic places for blocking off the marked-out sector for the party.

MILITARY OFFICER. Yes, go on.

ADC. I had just given the prisoner three or four solid squirts in the face and of course he was screaming like the civilian pig he is. I was about to close the door of the boot when they descended on the driver and myself. They spirited him away, sir and – er – rough-handled us.

MILITARY OFFICER (*begins pacing up and down*). Fill me in, fill me in. I still don't understand. You had your pistol, major. Why didn't you waste their ringleader? That's an elementary lesson you've been taught often enough. Waste the leader and the rabble will melt away.

ADC. If you will be good enough to observe, sir, I have been disarmed.

MILITARY OFFICER. You were . . . ?

ADC. Disarmed sir. We were grossly outnumbered.

MILITARY OFFICER. Don't talk rot, major! Our Intelligence report had fed us accurately with the strength of the Area Boys in this neighbourhood. An armed soldier is worth at least ten unarmed civilians any day, and there must have been at the very least . . .

ADC. Six of us, sir, counting the personnel in the escort car.

MILITARY OFFICER. Then what story are you trying to tell me? The Area Boys between the flyover and Ita Balogun number no more than sixty-three. That reduces the maximum number around this shopping centre to maybe twenty – make it twenty-four at the outside. Our Intelligence reports were detailed, right down to the muscular make-up of every Area thug. So will you please explain how six armed soldiers from the crack regiment were overwhelmed by twenty-four civilian rabble.

ADC (*points to the reflection in the sliding doors*). The Maroko rabble, sir. No Intelligence report alerted us to their presence here. They joined in, sir. They hemmed us in and cut us off all possible reinforcement. Our colleagues had no idea of what was happening. I doubt if they are aware of it up till now.

> MILITARY OFFICER, *now in a towering rage, strides up and down, slapping his swagger stick against his thighs. Stops, takes a look at his soldiers, grits his teeth and growls.*

MILITARY OFFICER. They shouldn't have done that. They shouldn't have tampered with your uniform. They should not have laid their hands on it. (*Thrusts his fists in the air.*) You should have warned them – DON'T TOUCH MY UNIFORM!!!

My uniform is sacrosant
From cap pom-pom to underpant
It cannot bear civilian touch
This cloth proclaims: you've met your match!
The uniform's forbidden grounds
For bloody civs. it's out-of-bounds
Don't get me mad, don't make me sore
Don't challenge my esprit-de-corps
    DON'T TOUCH MY UNIFORM!!!

Inflexible the starch foundation
A glossy boost to chest inflation
The pressing iron leaves on a crease
Of razor. Discipline guarantees
The buttons never lack for polish
Boots wear a gleam that women relish
And epaulettes stand stiff and spry

Straining as if to spring and fly
  DON'T TOUCH MY UNIFORM!!!

A private quarrel? Don't be coy
Our services you may employ
The sight of khaki makes all freeze
We'll take your side for a modest piece
Of the action paid in cash or kind
Just play the game and you will find
The uniform is the talisman
That proves that 'man pass man'
  DON'T TOUCH MY UNIFORM!!!

A Colonel at twenty-four
I've never been in any war
A leveller, that's a *coup-d'etat*
Makes room at the top for a third-rater
A very different breed we are
From foreign slaves to criteria
Like service, sense and competence
Or that bogus word – intelligence
  DON'T TOUCH MY UNIFORM!!!

The uniform means born to rule
The uniform marks the ultimate school.
Superior to the civic bounder
The uniform marks the all-rounder
Know-all, Be-all, Seize-all, End-all
Alpha and Omega, self install
As President and Head of State
Commander-in-Chief, Great Potentate
  DON'T TOUCH MY UNIFORM!!!
  DON'T TOUCH MY UNIFORM!!!
  JUST DO NOT TOUCH – MY UNIFORM!!!

(*His song over, he breathes heavily, then snaps to action.*) I don't
want just the traffic to be stopped. I am not interested in the
usual road blocks. I want this sector sealed up entirely. Not a

mouse goes in or out. Round up every moving object, anything that breathes, walks, looks or stinks like an Area Boy. Look in the local bars and pools shops. Break into the houses and the shops and flush them out. I want nothing less thorough than the Ogoni treatment. Do I make myself clear?

ADC. Orders clearly understood, sir.

MILITARY OFFICER. And that includes the Maroko migrants. They obviously haven't learned from this morning's exercise, so, we'll complete their lesson here. Those miserable items that they managed to salvage – smash them up. Pile them up and make a bonfire of them. If there's any resistance, don't be stingy with the bullets. I want a bonfire sunset here to rival the sunrise we donated to Maroko this morning. Let them know that the Army's fully in charge.

SANDA (*deferential cough to attract attention*). Colonel, sir, if I may put in a word . . .

MILITARY OFFICER. You may not, sir. I am in no mood for any plea for clemency. It's time we introduced some military discipline into these surroundings.

SANDA. Plea for clemency? From me, sir? You are just about to do the store a favour. These Area Boys are the very pestilence. They pester our clientele, intimidate them, extort money from them and vandalise their cars. You are about to make my job here much easier, I assure you, Colonel.

MILITARY OFFICER. Oh. At last some music to my ears. Yes, I'm listening. Play on.

SANDA. The wedding, sir. You're forgetting the wedding.

MILITARY OFFICER. No. I hadn't forgotten. I'm cleaning up the place for the wedding.

SANDA. You'll have a running battle on your hands, Colonel. I know them. I've seen them at work. Hit and run skirmishes will still be going on when the guests begin to arrive. The occasion will be totally marred and er . . . you, I rather suspect, you will be held responsible.

MILITARY OFFICER. Oh. (*Pauses.*) Hm. I must say . . . Maybe we should wait until the ceremony is over? It's expected to go on until dawn, you know.

SANDA. Of course. A dawn operation, just like Maroko. The Management will be particularly obliged to you.

MILITARY OFFICER (*thinks it over briefly*). That's it then. We'll concentrate on herding the Maroko invaders out of here. (*Gritting his teeth.*) In an orderly fashion – for now. If we have to, we'll even *plead* with them. But later, oh yes, later. Right! No further distractions – until dawn. Follow me!

> *They go off at a brisk pace, watched by BARBER and others. The MINSTREL plucks his box-guitar and sings: 'Maroko'. Towards the end, he is joined by others, including the passing evacuees.*

MINSTREL.

> Maroko o. What a ruckus
> Over a wretched shanty town.
> It was stinking
> It was sinking
> We were rescued or we would drown.
>
> The lagoon breeze was pestilence
> A miasma hung over the horizon.
> We were banished
> Or we'd be finished
> By sheer atmospheric poison.
>
> No electricity or piped water
> No sewage or garbage disposal.
> Was it decent
> To be indifferent?
> We must make way for urban renewal.
>
> Come learn from we new relocation
> The best nomadic architecture.
> Window or roof
> Like cattle on the hoof
> Will arrive some time in the future.

As for education for our children
Invention is the child of necessity.
In the open air
We'll pioneer
The genuine Open university.

So na here me I come relocate
With every modern amenity.
Food dey for belle
I even save my tele
Some day, we go get electricity.

Maroko! What an illusion
To make a home in the middle of the ocean
But the waters
Never hurt us
It was government with the Final Solution.

The light has been changing gradually to onset of dusk.
TRADER *enters with the departure of the soldiers, nods to*
SANDA *and begins to pack up his wares. So do* BARBER *and*
MAMA PUT *at a brisk pace. Enter a group of* SOLDIERS, *armed,*
aggressive. They charge the various stalls, throwing merch-
andise, pots and pans in every direction. Protestations. MAMA
PUT *goes wild, picks up her bayonet and dares them. Three*
guns are levelled at her. SANDA *finally makes himself heard*
during this stand-off.

SANDA. Cut it out! Did you hear me? I said, put those guns away!
   Do you realise you're disobeying the orders of your superior
   officer?
SOLDIER. Which officer? Our orders are to demolish all illegal
   structures.
SANDA. And I'm telling you the Colonel was here just now, and he
   expressly said that no stall around here was to be touched.
SOLDIER. Nobody mentioned any exceptions. Our orders were to
   tear down all illegal structures. Everything goes in the bonfire.

SANDA. I don't care what your orders were, but go ahead if you like. Go on, smash up one more item and see if you don't end up in the guardroom.

SOLDIER. But she tried to attack us. Look at her, still threatening my men with that knife. Nobody does that to my men and gets away with it!

SANDA. That's not a knife, you blind recruit. That's a bayonet. I told you she's an army wife. How else do you think she would be in possession of a bayonet? She has a gun too, you're lucky she chose not to use it.

SOLDIER (*cranes his neck to obtain a closer look*). Oh. It's a bayonet.

SANDA. Of course it's a bayonet. And she is an army wife. That's why the Colonel exempted this area. Now put everything back as you found it and I'll forget about this assault.

SOLDIER (*salutes* MAMA PUT). Sorry, ma'am. It was all a mistake. Thank you, sir. We'll put it all back. Come on, you two. Get moving.

> *They scamper round, trying to restore everything as before.*

MAMA PUT. Leave it, leave it. Just leave it and leave us alone. Go away. Get out of here!

SOLDIER. Sorry, ma'am. Very sorry. Squad, Fall out! (*They stumble out over one another, the leader making imploring gestures to* SANDA *to the last.*)

TRADER. As I bin say before, oga, you sabbe tink quick quick for your feet.

BARBER. Mama Put, so you done become army wife now. Which barracks make we come dey look for you?

> MAMA PUT *simmers down slowly, begins to repack up her things.*

SANDA. If you're going home to change for the party, you'd better get cracking yourself.

BARBER. Me, I don't need much time. A quick wash and a new

agbada, and no one can tell the difference between me and a retired General. I tell you, an *agbada* is the greatest leveller in the history of clothing. Of course the material can make all the difference but, the difference doesn't show that much at night.

SANDA. You're thinking of changing your trade to tailoring? Don't take too long, everybody. You're all coming in on my invitation. I'm reserving a table for you right here so I can make sure you get served to bursting.

TRADER. Me, my stomach done ready since yesterday.

SANDA. How is Judge?

TRADER. Na bad ting dat gas wey dem put for in face. 'E still not fit see when I leave am for house na but different ting 'e done begin talk now. 'E say 'e done make de journey wey e tell me about, and at last 'e discover the colour of the soul, and na pitch black 'e be. But e say 'e no sure if na in own soul 'e see, or that of Lagos, or even that of the whole nation. But everything there, e say na black with small small spots.

MINSTREL *sings: 'Ka L'owo L'owo, Kaa R'ayafe'.*

In a series of fussless, well coordinated moves:
The cleaners enter, sweep. Others begin to erect a marquee.
A carpet is rolled from the interior of the store down the steps.
A high table is set up, with plush chairs. Guest tables follow.
The major-domo *indicates where they are to go – and that is seemingly among the audience. The tables make their way downstage, down the aisles and out of sight.*

A 'juju' band enters, with instruments. The BAND LEADER *pats the* MINSTREL *on the shoulder.*

BAND LEADER. Good talk, colleague, your choice couldn't be more appropriate. This is one wedding that doesn't lack for cash or clout. (*Goes up to* SANDA.) Hallo, friend.

SANDA. You're welcome.

BAND LEADER. You don't happen to know where we're to set up, do you? We're The Benders, from Ibadan.

SANDA. I know you. Your group will play from the balcony. I'll take you there myself.

> *He leads them off, using the exit to the side. From now on, the sliding doors will remain firmly closed. The preparations continue, with the workforce responding to the lyrics, joining in and giggling at the suggestive sections. The caterers enter with huge tureens, covered dishes, warmers and coolers. The band begins to tune up their instruments. Soon, they take up the MINSTREL's song and throw in their full instrumentation.*

> *The sliding doors reflect cars arriving, depositing GUESTS, driving off. SANDA returns. He has changed his uniform for a buba and soro. Strolls round to make routine checks, impassively. GUESTS arrive.*

> *Finally, the party of the BRIDEGROOM appears, heralded by a small combo of High Life musicians, led by a trumpeter. They are ushered to the High Table by the MASTER OF CEREMONIES. Once seated, he shoos off the group who disappear in the same direction as the 'juju' band, whose music again resurfaces in the background.*

> *A siren tears the evening apart, and a convoy of cars is reflected in the sliding doors. Car doors opening, stamp of boots etc. The MASTER OF CEREMONIES nearly falls on his face as he rushes to the foot of the steps to usher in the august guest. A few moments later and a portly figure in uniform, brimming with medals ascends the steps and is duly placed at the head of the table, his ADC standing at attention behind him. The table rises to scrape and bow. The band strikes up the national anthem and all stand at attention. The MC is beside himself.*

MC. Your Excellency the Military Governor, your Excellencies honourable members of the diplomatic corps, my Lords spiritual and temporal, your Royal Highnesses the Emirs, Obis, Obas, Chiefs and other titled dignitaries, revered families of the Bride

and Bridegroom, friends of the families of Bride and Bridegroom, distinguished guests, ladies and gentlemen, and all other
protocols observed, it is my great honour and privilege to
formally declare open this engagement ceremony between the
illustrious families of Chief Honourable Surveyor Kingboli, BSc.
Cantab., Order of Merit, honorary doctorates and chieftaincy
titles too numerous to mention – and Professor Sematu, BA,
MA, DSc., former Minister of Oil and Petroleum Resources and
Ambassador Extraordinary to many nations in his long and
illustrious career. Please put your hands together for the living
heads of these two families, whom God has spared to be among
us on this august occasion to witness the sealing of the bond of
happiness between their charming offsprings. Put your hands
together please.

> *Enthusiastic clapping, accompanied by fanfare.* MC *gestures
> to the two family heads to rise and take a bow. They do.*

Your Excellencies, my Lords Temporal, distinguished guests,
ladies and gentlemen, all other protocols observed. Although my
humble self will be taking charge of the proceedings, it is
necessary at this stage to announce and welcome the chairman of
the occasion. Yes, we dared invite. Yes, we dared our interme-
diaries. Yes, we dared nurse expectations. Yes, we dared trepi-
dations. Yes, we dared anticipate and yes, we dared hope and
behold – his Excellency is here in person, the Honourable
Military Governor of Lagos State . . . (*Clapping. Fanfare. The*
MILITARY GOVERNOR *rises, and acknowledges.*) Your Excellency, it is an honour. On behalf of both families, I thank you
profoundly for taking time off your busy schedule to honour us
with your presence at this ceremony, and even more, to preside
over the occasion.

Your Excellency the Chairman, honourable members of the
diplomatic corps, my Lords Temporal and Spiritual, all other
protocols observed. As we proceed, I shall have the honour to

recognise some of our distinguished guests — yes, the list increases all the time, and I promise that all necessary recognitions will duly take place. However, I regret to say that, thanks to the crisis in the nation, fomented by some disgruntled elements, his Excellency our Chairman is obliged to take a plane to Abuja this very evening for an emergency meeting of the Armed Forces Ruling Council. His time with us is therefore very short, and without further ado, we shall proceed to the heart of the business that has brought us here tonight. Needless to say, it is an all night affair for the rest of us who do not have to keep watchful vigil on the affairs of the nation. We shall carry on till daybreak. You will notice that at the bottom of your invitation cards, are the initials RSVP. Well, for those of you who do not know what that means, it simply says:

GUESTS. Rice and Stew Very Plenty.

MC. Need I say more? And of course, that other one which is taken for granted — Bar . . .

GUESTS. Inexhaustable.

MC. This is obviously a highly sophisticated gathering, which is only to be expected. And now . . . (*Signals towards the balcony. Fanfare.*) Please put your hands together for the bridegroom.

> BRIDEGROOM's *entry, accompanied by drummer. He is followed by an attendant who carries an outsize briefcase. He stops at the foot of the steps.* MC *signals the band to stop.*

Stop! Wait a minute. What is this? Ladies and gentlemen, I think we have a little mystery here. This is not an office. The bridegroom is not going on a business trip. Our son is not absconding. He is not attending a board meeting. I thought we had all been invited to his betrothal. That he should arrive with a basket of kolanuts would be in order. That he should be trailed by bolts of *akwete* cloth would be no surprise. That he should be trailed by a lorry load of male yams, palm oil and bags of salt would be answering true to his origin. Or cases of *oyinbo* wine and champagne — why not? Don't we know that he was trained in

Toronto, Paris, and Budapest? So why not? But a briefcase! I am bewildered, mystified, confounded, disconcerted, and discombobulated.

Cries of 'More! More! Fire on! Finish the vocab!' Plus applause.

Ladies and gentlemen, I think we are about to witness something rarer than the sight of an elephant giving birth. We are about witness the secrets of the other side of the moon. At the end of a fruitless hunt, we sighed and got ready to make do with a wild tuber. When we pulled it from the hot ashes what did we find? A whole roast antelope! And they say the age of miracle makers is gone? We plunged our calabash into the animal's drinking hole and found it filled with frothing palm wine. They told us there were no leaves on the tree because it was harmattan, but they had reckoned without the perennial rain tree. Undoubted son of your father, do as your father has been known to do! Outdo your ancestors as your father did in his time! If you see me tomorrow morning with lockjaw, say I brought it on myself. Say it was I who said to the miracle masquerade: Surprise me!

With an indolent motion, the BRIDEGROOM *reaches into the briefcase with the left hand, pulls out a fistful of naira notes, scatters them on the carpet behind him as he ascends each step. The* GUESTS *go wild, the drummer ecstatic. He repeats this all the way to the top, so that the carpet is overlaid with another carpet of banknotes. When he reaches the high table, he bows. The table rises to greet him, led by the* MILITARY GOVERNOR *who even throws him a salute.*

The BRIDEGROOM *then proceeds to the bench placed to one side for his party, again carpeting the way behind him with notes. Takes his seat to thunderous applause. The attendant turns the briefcase upside down, waves it above his head to show it has been emptied.*

The MOTHER OF THE DAY *has taken the place of the* MASTER OF CEREMONIES.

MOTHER OF THE DAY. Enh, forgive me, our elders, but it was the cockatoo who pecked too deep inside iroko wood pursuing a worm, that is why its beak is bent till today. You see me here because that man who was here before, jeered that there were no more tricks in the masquerade's pouch. The masquerade said, 'Turn your head and look behind you.' The man turned to look but he saw nothing unusual. 'I don't see anything,' he said. 'That's the trick,' said the masquerade. Till today, you can encounter the man still walking about with his head turned this way, the rest of his body that way. When he recovers, he'll be back with us. Meanwhile, well, the fact that the drum is at rest doesn't mean that the legs won't tap. The rhythm of yesterday still lingers in the head of the trained dancer, and this gathering with all due respect, contains some of the best trained citizens of this nation – you only have to look at the quality of the presence we have on our high table, and all around.

Yes, that rhythm. Our dear Excellency the Chairman and Military governor, ladies and gentlemen, I dare say that you may have missed something when our prime young elephant showed his mettle on the way to take his place. Did it not seem contrary to familiar usage? Our forefathers say that the wise one always throws his water forwards because whoever moistens the ground before him will surely tread fruitful earth. And don't we all pray to place our feet on earth that is bursting with fruit? But our young son kept nourishing the ground behind him. Now, I ask you, what could that mean? Is he being chased by hired assassins or armed robbers? Was that a way to slow them down? Or did he think he was on his village farm where you walk backwards to sow the guinea corn? Or could it be – yes, I wonder, I wonder with delicious anxiety – could it just be that he – that he, he is laying a trail for someone to follow. A trail that must lead eventually to himself. A trail of love. Of devotion. A trail of – shall I say it? Shall I seat it on the ground and seal it with a prayer? A trail of . . . *omo jojolo*. Of children, and grandchildren, and great grandchildren . . . ?

Fanfare. Enter the BRIDE, *with attendants. The* GUESTS *rise. She steps on the carpet of notes all the way to the high table. She turns to the right, as if about to follow the trail of money but is stopped by the* MOTHER OF THE DAY.

MOTHER OF THE DAY. No, miss! Over there.

She is led to the opposite bench. The MOTHER OF THE DAY *feigns displeasure.*

Hng-ngh-ngh! I don't know what is wrong with the children of this modern age. Did you see that? She couldn't wait. She just couldn't wait. I have a mind to send her back to the village where she can be properly educated. (*Laughter. The* BRIDE *is seated.*) That's better. If you are in a hurry, we are not. If you and your hus . . . sorry o, you see, even I have caught the hurry-hurry disease. Yes, if you and your – intended – are thinking of packing up the food and drinks to stock your new home, you've got another think coming. We are not leaving here until the last drop has been drunk and the last speck of food licked off the plate. When we are done, you will think that an army of soldier ants invaded this place because when we've given you away – *if* we do give you away – we don't know when next we shall be invited to see the contents of your soup-pot. Now – (*She signals offstage. A maid appears with a well polished gourd and calabash cup, places it down before the* BRIDE.) Well, there it is. I hope it is not too heavy for you to carry. It had better not be, because you'll be carrying something heavier before long – that's if you are not carrying it already. One never knows. After all we seem to live in a hurry-hurry age.

I hope you know what to do. There are your parents. There are all these witnesses, all men and women of – as we say – timber and calibre. Let's go. (BRIDE *rises. The attendants place the gourd in her arms.*) We've only heard that there is a man who wants you for a bride – as if there is anything surprising about that – but we don't know him. We don't even know what he's like. All we know is that he must have a good pair of eyes in his head. There – (*She waves towards the audience.*) – as you see, there are plenty of fishes in the sea. Go and see if your man is there. When you start pouring him a drink, we'll know that he is no stranger.

Band: 'Meta Meta L'ore o'.

BRIDE *comes down the steps and scans the faces of the audience. Entering into the game, she makes a pretence of being about to set down the gourd before one man, then another, but veers off at the last moment, teasing the victim. Festive reactions as she feints off each expectation. She returns to the* MOTHER OF THE DAY, *shaking her head negatively.*

MOTHER OF THE DAY. What? No sign of him there? Well, some people are really choosy, I must say. Oh, I see. Sometimes, you know, we miss the obvious. I had forgotten we had some real cream of society seated over there. (*Points at the high table.*) All right, so that's where he is enh? Go and serve him his palm wine so we can all go home. I'm getting tired of all this and you're keeping us from the food and drinks.

The smiling BRIDE-TO-BE *goes to the High Table, scans all the faces, looks closely at the the* ADC, *frowns and shakes her head, then makes to set down the gourd in front of the* MILITARY GOVERNOR. *Mock horror from the* MILITARY GOVERNOR. *She glides smoothly away just before the gourd touches the table. Applause. She returns to the* MOTHER OF THE DAY. *She waves her off 'angrily', goes and plonks herself in the* BRIDE's *seat.*

MOTHER OF THE DAY. No. I have nothing more to do with you? We've looked at everybody and still you're not satisfied. Am I now to put an advertisement in the papers to find someone suitable for you? Or start combing farmsteads and thorough-fares? Or travel overseas – oh yes, maybe you're one of those who dream of marrying a foreigner. A white man. You think we don't have enough milk in our cocoa, not so? (BRIDE *stands forlornly before her*.) Well, don't just stand there like a drenched chicken. Look around and see if there is any rooster hiding in some corner of the barn. Sleeping, maybe. Or hiding. Playing hard to get. Or maybe he thinks it's him we're planning to slaughter and serve up to our guests. Of course there is also the military around. Maybe he thinks they're here to whisk him away into detention. The poor creature is probably frightened to death. Starving. Thirsty. See if you can find him and revive him with a drink. Don't come back here until you've found him!

> *The* BRIDE *goes off, follows the money trail. As she reaches the High Table, she appears to slow down, pauses, looks in the direction of the* BRIDEGROOM. *She walks slowly in his direction. A roll of drums begins softly, welling up. She reaches the* BRIDEGROOM, *begins to set down the gourd. Just before it touches the ground, she straightens up again and turns around. The* BRIDEGROOM *smiles broadly – it's all still part of the game. His supporters tease him, and the* GUESTS *applaud. The* MOTHER OF THE DAY *turns to the High Table and audience in a mock appeal.*

> *Only gradually is the change of expression on* MISEYI's *face noticed. It has become set. She comes down the steps, looks slowly around, then breaks into a run.* SANDA *is the most surprised person when she runs up to him, plonks down the gourd before him and turns round defiantly to face the High Table.*

> *For a few moments there is stunned silence. Then the* BRIDE-GROOM *leaps up, breathing heavily.*

TRADER (*dolefully*). Sai! E done sele! I done warn oga make e get ready to dodge. As I watch how dat woman dey yap am dis morning, enh . . .

BRIDEGROOM. This – is an insult! This – is an unpardonable insult!

CHIEF KINGBOLI (*incoherent with rage*). Who – is – that – man?

MILITARY GOVERNOR (*leaping up*). Arrest him! (MILITARY GOVERNOR's ADC *leaps into action.*)

MISEYI. What for?

CHIEF KINGBOLI. My family has been insulted. Publicly insulted.

BRIDEGROOM. I want him castrated.

> MILITARY GOVERNOR's ADC *advances towards the couple,* MISEYI *standing protectively in front of* SANDA. TRADER, BARBER *and* MAMA PUT *emerge and surround them.* TRADER *puts his fingers to his lips and lets off a loud whistle. A stand-off between* ADC *and the group.*

CHIEF KINGBOLI (*rounds on* MISEYI's *father*). You were in the know. You planned to humiliate me in public. You've never forgotten that oil contract you lost to my company.

MILITARY GOVERNOR (*panicky*). No, not here. Not in public.

CHIEF KINGBOLI. Why not? Because you backed him in cabinet? I knew you had an interest in his firm but I won the contract anyway. He's never forgiven or forgotten, neither had you. So you both plotted to inflict this disgrace on my family?

MILITARY GOVERNOR. S-sh! Stop it! Let's go to my residence and sort this out. Let's all keep a cool head.

CHIEF KINGBOLI. Just remember I have friends and partners among your superiors!

MILITARY GOVERNOR (*places his arms round him*). Let's go, let's go. You've got it all wrong. I am just as shocked . . .

BRIDEGROOM. All I want is to see him castrated. Publicly!

MILITARY GOVERNOR (*seeing the stand-off at the* MISEYI *end*). Send for reinforcements, Major!

> *From under her wrapper,* MAMA PUT *whips out her bayonet.* ADC *freezes. The* MILITARY GOVERNOR *stares aghast.*

Confusion as the GUESTS *scatter. The* MILITARY GOVERNOR
knocks back his chair, and moves down.

Leave them be. Let's go. We'll deal with them later. Get the
outriders started. (ADC *salutes and runs out.*) Come on, gentlemen, to my residence. Let's go over this in my place calmly. It's a
family affair, so let's stay calm. This is the time to keep our
heads. Let's talk family to family. We'll all ride in my convoy.

BRIDEGROOM (*follows the High Table* GUESTS. *Signals to his
retinue to gather up the money*). Pick up every last naira.

TRADER (*steps forward and wags his finger*). Oh-oh.

BRIDEGROOM (*hesitates. But the* MILITARY GOVERNOR's *party is
already out of sight. Turns to* SANDA). You'll need it. You'll need
it for your medical bills. Because if it's the last thing I do in this
world, I'll cut off your genitals!

BARBER. Did you hear that? With all his money, he still wants to
make more – and using his rival's genitals!

BRIDEGROOM *storms off. Several moments silence.*

SANDA (*sighs*). I do not recall proposing.

MISEYI. Neither do I.

SANDA. I am not prepared for marriage.

MISEYI. Neither am I.

SANDA. So what the hell did you do that for?

MISEYI. As the something said to the other, it seemed a good idea at
the time.

SANDA. So what happens now?

MISEYI (*facing him*). Well, there is a feast.

SANDA. The guests are gone.

MISEYI. Oh, I don't think so. Trader.

TRADER. Yes, Miss Bride.

MISEYI. Do you think this feast will be wasted for want of guests?

TRADER. I get locusts plenty for outside, miss. Save for food or
drink to waste, na dem belle go burst.

SANDA. You'd better first take care of that money, Trader. We've
got to store it up rightaway. I'm not sure even I can control the

boys if they set eyes on it, and it's got to be given back. Barber,
Boyko . . .

They begin sweeping up the money, joined by MAMA PUT.

TRADER. Enh? You say we go give 'am back, oga?

MISEYI. No, he didn't mean that.

SANDA. I do. It's not yours.

MISEYI (*sighs*). I forgot, these differences in cultures. Among my
people, tradition makes the money – mine. For us, that is asking
money. It is show-off money. It isn't bride price or dowry or
anything like that. It enters the bride's home, and it stays there
whatever the answer is. It can be one coin, one yam tuber, some
woven cloth or jewellery, or a wad of tobacco. None of that is
refundable. It's like the running expenses for the ceremony.

SANDA. But what on earth made you change your mind. I thought
you were all set for domestic bliss. The merging of two powerful
dynasties.

MISEYI. I don't know. I just knew I couldn't go through with it.
Look, let's talk of more serious business. I know what you think
you've been doing, I approve, but I think you've been going it the
wrong way. Look at Boyko for instance, he should be in school.

SANDA. As a matter of fact, I've been giving it some thought. I've
been reshaping my ideas lately, it's just that no sooner does one
appear to see light, than a new cloud of questions obscures one's
vision. Look at Maroko today. What answer does one have to
that? What remedy does one apply? Before a new crisis is over,
another has been hatched. Before Maroko it was . . . wait one
second!

MISEYI. What is it?

SANDA. Get a move on, Trader. Quick, quick, everybody! They'll
be back. You bet they'll be back. Once they've escorted the
governor home safely, they'll be back. And that colonel, when he
gets to hear about what happened here – and he's probably being
briefed at this very moment . . . Come on, come on! Not a
moment to lose. Get all the food and drinks into the banqueting

room. It's soundproofed and air-conditioned. (*Stops and thinks fast. Looks around.*) Here, Boyko . . .

BOYKO. Yes, Mr Sanda.

SANDA (*grabs a fistful of notes and gives it to him*). You'll stay behind. They must find a pile of this with you – you know what to do. They'll snatch it off you. You'll burst into tears. You'll plead with them, saying that it's all you were left by the Area Boys who grabbed the rest of the loot. Now where did they go with it? Where?

BOYKO. I heard them say they were going to Anikulapo's nightclub to celebrate.

SANDA. Can't you think of somewhere much further off?

BOYKO. The Good Time Bar in Ikorodu.

SANDA. Good lad! Just sit there in all innocence and play on that flute.

MISEYI. Sanda!

SANDA. He'll go to school, I've promised. This is just a routine service for his old school. A last service, sure. No use wasting acquired skills. My friend Barber, can you handle the police bit?

BARBER. Trust me. You want the Kill-and-Go, the Mobile?

SANDA. None other. Those ones with permanent fire in their eyes and holes in their pockets. Use the basement entrance when you get back.

BARBER *goes off.*

MISEYI. Now what was that all about?

SANDA. Greed. Rivalry. Barber will lodge a formal complaint to the police that some soldiers made off with a few hundred thousands from the party and have gone to celebrate at the Good Time Bar. After the clash, there will be the usual commission of enquiry.

MISEYI. My God. Is this all you have been learning since you abandoned college?

SANDA. No. It's the way I've learnt to apply all I learnt. Both in there where we both were, and out here. Outside is one great learning place, Miseyi.

MISEYI (*the penny finally drops. She looks shocked. Turns slowly to inspect* TRADER *and the few remaining hangers-on more carefully*). Wait a minute. I know what you've become. You are not just a *megadi*, not just a security guard. You are one of them. An Area Boy. King of the Area Boys!

SANDA (*bowing*). At your service – if you prefer to put it that way.

MISEYI. Those bullies? Enforcers and extortionists? Thugs, yes, sheer thugs. Ready to serve the highest bidder. They make potholes in the middle of the road, then extort money from motorists for their – public spirited – service in filling them up. They break your windscreen if you don't pay up or slash your tyres. They rip the necklace off your neck in a traffic hold-up or snatch your watch. They're robbers. Daylight robbers. No better than armed robbers. That's the kind of people you consort with? Or is it worse? How much further have you sunk? Drugs? Cocaine pushing? Tell me the lot, what else?

SANDA. No-o-o, I am not that far up on the social ladder. Certainly not on the same rung as your father, or your would-be father-in-law for that matter. You heard them and the Military Governor at their bickering. I am not a pen robber. I don't lift oil illegally. I have never traded off import licences and I have never looted the treasury.

MISEYI. You dare impute . . . !

SANDA (*quietly*). I do.

> MISEYI *bristles, then wilts. She plonks herself down on the steps.*

Let's face it. You didn't meet me after all these years and fall in love with me. You fled your fiancé with the gourd because I reminded you of the values you once held. When you were not afraid to admit or speak the truth about anything – including your family. I don't say I am right in everything I've done since then but, we did remind each other of a little of our real selves. Wasn't that what really happened?

MISEYI. Oh, I am confused. What do we do now?

SANDA. First, move into safety. I am sorry, but I'm used to being practical. I have become used to having many people in my charge, and their welfare comes first. The heavier issues of the nation must wait for now, there'll be plenty of time to discuss them. Let's join the others in the banqueting hall.

MISEYI. Is it safe?

SANDA. I'm in charge of the plaza.

MISEYI. But what's the use of a wedding banquet without a wedding? I don't really feel like partying for the sake of partying.

SANDA. We-e-e-ll, I've been doing some thinking. (*Pulls her up.*)

MISEYI. But now you don't even have a job. I hope you realise that.

SANDA. I see you also have been doing some thinking.

MISEYI (*pulling sharply away*). I am not in love with you. What I did then was just – just – impulse. Sheer impulse.

SANDA (*puts his arms around her and leads her upstage*). I know. I've just had an impulsive idea myself. We could settle down with the Maroko people in one of the new locations. It will be cheap, and we would be among the founding members. There will be a lot of demand on us. We could work with them, take up their case, maybe get them compensation – that at least . . .

MISEYI. And what do we live on in the meantime?

SANDA. We-e-ell, to tell you the truth. I was already planning to leave this job. Leave this place altogether. I know I was searching for solutions but, well, this isn't it. So, I've been quietly putting a band together. We can eke out a reasonable living from that.

MISEYI. From subversive music? Because I can already guess . . .

SANDA. Come on, of course we'll diversify. The right music for the right occasion. Maybe you'll even pick up the old xylophone and join the band. But the real work will be with Maroko, not just that Maroko, but the Maroko all around, the eternal nightmare of a Maroko into which one wakes every day.

MISEYI. What can one do with the military still around?

SANDA. They won't always be there.

MISEYI. Who is going to remove them?

SANDA. You see, there is already plenty for us to think about. And plan towards. And two heads are better than one . . .

MISEYI. I've always wanted to found something worthwhile.

SANDA. Well, here's your chance. Why don't we go in and raise a toast to that?

> *They go off in the same direction as the others. Except for* BOYKO *playing his flute, the stage is empty. Enter* JUDGE, *in dark glasses. He listens.*

JUDGE. Who's in there?

BOYKO. Just me, Judge. (JUDGE *turns, and stumbles against a chair.*) Careful, Judge. Are you all right?

JUDGE. Fairly so. Fairly so. Just the little mystery of these wandering souls. I was certain I'd caught up with mine at last, and it was a void without features, mottled as the conscience of a tyrant. I know him by the way. I was locked up in the boot of a car but I heard them talking. Before I was gassed. What didn't they do to Maroko! Boastful bastards! So it was they who faked that sunrise. Dislodged a million people to rival my own labour of the spirit. Damn! I was so sure it was my own handiwork.

BOYKO. You don't seem all right.

JUDGE. It's getting light again, as if they've all begun to reform. But that I'll believe when I see it.

BOYKO. Oh. You must leave quickly, Uncle. The soldiers will be back any time.

JUDGE. Animals!

BOYKO. Judge, you must hurry.

JUDGE. I close the book of the prerogative of mercy against them. And their kind who masquerade in sheep's clothing. For ever!

BOYKO. Come, Judge, I think I can hear them already. Hurry!

JUDGE. Where to? Has this not always been our space?

BOYKO. Mr Sanda says you must come with me. At once.

JUDGE. That's different. That Security man appears to know what's what. A very sensible young man.

Snatching up the pile of notes, BOYKO *rushes him up the steps.
As they reach the level of the High Table, soldiers break into
the area.*

SOLDIER. Stop!

BOYKO. Come on, Judge!

A shot rings out. JUDGE *pitches forward, falls.*

Judge!

SOLDIER *(gun levelled at* BOYKO*).* You! Come here!

BOYKO *looks down on the prone figure of* JUDGE *and hesitates.*

If you don't want to join him, you'd better bring yourself here.

BOYKO *(slowly raises his arms, the money held in both hands).*
Why did you have to shoot him? Judge has never harmed . . .

SOLDIER. Shut up! I said, com . . . *(His eyes pop.)* What's that
you've got in your hands?

BOYKO *(sniffing).* That's all they left him, and me.

SOLDIER *(moving on him).* Who? Where's the rest? And where are
the others? *(Snatches the money. The others crowd round them.)*

BOYKO. They went off to celebrate. They took everything.

SOLDIER. Where? Come on, you wretched little thug? Where did
they go?

BOYKO. I heard one say The Good Time Bar, Ikorodu. They said
they wanted to get as far away from here as they could.

SOLDIER *(shoves him violently away).* Let's go. Move it, move it!

They rush out. SANDA *looks in round the corner. Enters,
followed by* MISEYI, TRADER, MAMA PUT, BARBER *etc.*

SANDA. What happened? We heard a shot.

BOYKO *(weeping).* They killed him. They shot him in the back.

JUDGE *(groans).* Here I go again. In the kingdom of lost souls.

BOYKO. Judge, are you still breathing?

MISEYI. Oh, thank goodness. We must get him to a hospital.

SANDA *rushes to his side. Kneels and turns him over. Examines
him.*

SANDA. He's not bleeding. Judge, what happened?

JUDGE. Someone knocked me down, gave me a powerful blow on the back.

SANDA. What's this? (*He feels under the robe and exposes some thick, quilted material. Props him up into a sitting position.*) He didn't have this on when he left. Judge, where did you find this?

JUDGE. The waistcoat? In the boot of the car where they locked me. I've always wanted a waistcoat to go with the robe. It should be black of course, a judicial black, with a golden chain. I've had the chain hidden away for a long time, but not all my foraging could turn up a waistcoat – until I found myself in the boot. Not much to do in there, so I poked around. Foraging becomes a habit you know, and there is plenty of room in a Mercedes boot. You'd be astonished what other items I discovered.

SANDA (*he has taken off the robe and the waistcoat. Holds up the latter. Shakes his head, laughing*). This is a bullet-proof vest, do you realise that? A bullet-proof vest! You lead a charmed life, Judge, that's all I can say.

JUDGE. Bullet-proof? (*Feels himself frantically.*) You mean I'm not dead? I thought I was already at destination. I must confess I was rather pleased to find you all there. I never doubted you. I was certain none of you lacked soul, it was only a matter of finding out where it was hidden. (*Struggling up. Winces.*) My back is sore.

SANDA. You're lucky it's no worse. Come. I'll bring you where the others are. The programme has changed slightly, but the party continues till daybreak.

JUDGE (*as he is led off*). Ah yes, daybreak. Another sunrise to plan, this time, make it foolproof, keep those vandals from interfering and rivalling my prerogative with a bestial conflagration . . . I shall never forgive them. Never!

> TRADER *groans and disappears with* BARBER *ahead of the others.* MINSTREL's *voice in the distance, singing: 'B'orombo Ta Bo'. The band joins in. The set is left empty.*

GLOSSARY

agabada	loose traditional gown (male)
akara	bean cake
akwete	a locally woven cloth
alawada	clown
bosikana	food-shack
buba	loose female blouse
ewa	bean
gari	farina
haba	come on!
juju	magic, supernatural powers
kain-kain	distilled palm-wine (usually around 80% proof)
konkere	bean pottage with farina
megadi	security guard
molue	locally built passenger bus
oga	boss
omo jojolo	treasured child
omolanke	locally made, commercial luggage cart
oyinbo	white man
patapata	absolutely, entirely
saka-jojo	shadow-play; silent film
sapagiri	prison version of konkere (*see above*)
sawa-sawa	whitebait (peppered)
so-o-say	problem-free
soro	straight-leg trousers
wahala	trouble
wayo	fraud, con game

TRANSLATIONS FOR PRISONERS' SONGS

Left – Right – Left. Left – Right – Left.
Be it warder, be it prisoner
Both of them are one.
Be it soldier, or policeman
Irredeemable thieves
Who gets caught is the one we browbeat
The real thief's on the loose.
The robber is dressed in khaki
The General a robber
The Major a bandit
Slaps you round and snatches your wife
Twists your arm and seizes your home
Bribery left, corrupt right
Your place is reserved right here
Your place in the prison yard
Left – Right – Left. Left – Right – Left.

Left – Right – Left. Left – Right – Left.
The river is fearless. Left – Right. I'm in goal
Left – Right. I have climbed up, I have plunged
Faka–fiki faka fi
The forest depths are nothing, the savanna holds no surprise
Does the bridge not leap over the gorge?
Watch the prisoner leap over his days
I have gone in, I've collected my number
The bean pottage is firm in my stomach
Be it the river, be it the ocean
The wind leaps over them both
The railway merely boasts; there is nothing new to the eye
The Sanitary Inspector is a liar
The dungheap is ever a dungheap.
Mosquito larvae still inhabit the waterpot
Even if you strain harder than the last year
Left – Right – Left. Left – Right – Left.
Soldier politician, incorrigible robber
Father of mayhem, you no longer bear arms
You fight no wars but chase contracts all over the place.

www.ingramcontent.com/pod-product-compliance
Ingram Content Group UK Ltd.
Pitfield, Milton Keynes, MK11 3LW, UK
UKHW040639280225
455688UK00001B/7

9 780413 686800